JOHN HULBERT was brought up in St Andrews, a
medicine in Edinburgh. He worked first in medi
then was a general practitioner for over 30 years
wife, Sara, in the Perthshire village of Longforga

Elected to Perth & Kinross Council in 1995, he served as Provost
from 2007 to 2012. As Provost he coordinated Perth's 800th
anniversary celebrations, and led the successful campaign to restore
City Status, which had been unceremoniously removed in 1975.

He is active in several Perth organisations, being chairman of
the Friends of St John's Kirk of Perth, an Honorary Fellow of the
Royal Scottish Geographical Society, an Honorary Friend of the
Black Watch Castle and Museum, and an Officer of the Order of
St John. In 2013 the President of Poland awarded him the Knight's
Cross of the Order of Merit of the Republic of Poland, for
developing good relations between Perth and Poland.

Drawing on the knowledge he gained as Provost, he published
Perth: A Comprehensive Guide for Locals and Visitors in 2014. It
was the first illustrated guide book for Perth.

*John Hulbert's guide to Perth is a magnificent combination of historical
analysis and contemporary appreciation of our fine City. It is an invaluable
book, written with such care and precision by a former Provost, who led the
effort to restore Perth to its rightful place as a city of Scotland.*
JOHN SWINNEY, MSP

Scotland's oldest and newest city

How Perth Regained its City Status and Why it Matters

John Hulbert

Luath Press Limited
EDINBURGH
www.luath.co.uk

First published 2016

ISBN: 978-1-910745-76-2

The paper used in this book is recyclable. It is made from
low chlorine pulps produced in a low energy, low emissions manner
from renewable forests.

Printed and bound by
CPI Antony Rowe, Chippenham

All images by John Hulbert except where otherwise stated

Typeset in 8.5 point Sabon by
3btype.com

*For the People of Perth whose
whole hearted commitment to the
City Status project ensured its success.*

Foreword

The securing (or as John Hulbert would always remind us) the 'restoring' of Perth's City Status was one of the most important events in the recent history of Perth. It was a campaign that engaged the whole city and involved the majority of the city's communities and organisations. John Hulbert led from the front as Provost of Perth and Kinross Council, putting the case with quiet determination, convincing persuasiveness, but most of all with his conviction of the 'right' of Perth to join the elite community of Scotland's cities.

Perth's bid for this honour was fired by the historic injustice of having our city status so arbitrarily withdrawn during the local authority reorganisation in 1975, compounded by observing other large towns in Scotland securing city title honours. It was also about civic ambition and the determination of a community to recognise its rightful place as a significant and serious participant in our nation's civic architecture.

In this book, John Hulbert contextualises the ups and downs of our attempt to secure City Status. He takes us back to the days when Perth was the ancient capital of Scotland and chronicles its role as Scotland's Second City during the creation and crafting of modern Scotland. It is from these deep historic roots that we better understand Perth's claim. The prevarication about the city competition and the basis of how the contest would be assessed are also described in detail, as well as how the strategy, that would bring Perth eventual success, was developed.

It is the sections on the sheer scale of activity in the run up to the contest where John Hulbert brings the campaign to life. The celebrations around Perth's 800th Anniversary and the national Homecoming were particularly important in promoting the city throughout Scotland and the UK. The engaging of Scotland's wider political community and the co-operation that was secured when we became Scotland's sole candidate are also recognised as key factors in Perth's eventual success.

Perth's City Status is now rightfully restored and the opportunities that are bequeathed are now for those who live and work in Scotland's newest official city. We go forward with a new campaign to become the UK's 'city' of culture and see the Stone of Destiny rightly returned to Perthshire. These challenges are made all the easier because we are again a recognised city and we have John Hulbert to thank for getting us here through his diligent leadership of this campaign.

Pete Wishart MP

Contents

	Acknowledgements	8
	Preface	9
CHAPTER ONE	Introduction	11
CHAPTER TWO	Ancient Capital of Scotland	14
CHAPTER THREE	History of City Status in the United Kingdom	29
CHAPTER FOUR	Developing the Strategy	37
CHAPTER FIVE	The first application and the Westminster dinner	61
CHAPTER SIX	2010 – The year of Perth800: Civic Events	72
CHAPTER SEVEN	Building the momentum for City Status	109
CHAPTER EIGHT	The second application	132
CHAPTER NINE	Unexpected Government 'U' Turn	139
CHAPTER TEN	The Final Push	142
CHAPTER ELEVEN	City Status Achieved: The Announcement, The Celebrations and The Award	148
CHAPTER TWELVE	Unfinished Business – the Lord Provostship	159
CHAPTER THIRTEEN	The Legacy	165
CHAPTER FOURTEEN	Beyond City Status	171
	Index	185

Acknowledgements

First of all I would like to thank Mr Pete Wishart MP for agreeing to write a Foreword for this book. Since he was first elected in 2001 Pete has been a staunch advocate for Perth and Perthshire. During the City Status campaign he was our eyes and ears in London, keeping us abreast of developments which might influence the result.

I am especially grateful to Angus Findlay, who is a particularly skilled photographer. He has contributed many photographs to the book, especially of the military events which took place during my five years as Provost. Without his pictures, the book would be bereft indeed.

Other local photographers and many organisations have been very willing to allow me to use their photographs. While they are all acknowledged in the text, I wish to state here how grateful I am for their cooperation.

I am very indebted to *The Courier* and the *Perthshire Advertiser*. As well as allowing me to use their photographs, the enthusiastic support which both gave to City Status contributed to the lift in Perth's morale which shone through the campaign, and was an important factor in its success.

Much of the information about Perth's history, and the legal status of the City and Lord Provost was acquired during my time as provost. Among those who were a great help at that time and since is Steve Connelly, Perth's long standing archivist, Ian Innes, formerly Head of Legal Services (both now retired) and David Strachan of the Perth & Kinross Heritage Trust.

My thanks are also due staff at the AK Bell Library and the Perth Museum and Art Gallery and especially to Christine Wood, Paul Adair and Rhona Rodger for advice and permission to reproduce images of some important paintings and artefacts.

Above all, however, my thanks are due to my wife, Sara, for her forbearance during the research and writing of this, my second book about Perth. She was the first to read each part of the book, and her advice shaped much of its development. And so the book is dedicated to her with love and respect.

Preface

Perth800 and the Civic Honours Campaign

The loss of prestige when Perth's City Status was abolished in 1975 hurt deeply. Perth had always been a city at the heart of Scotland, geographically, politically and commercially. Kenneth MacAlpin, the first King of Scots, established his Kingdom at Scone in 843AD and had his palace at Forteviot. Perth, with its bridge and harbour, was the knot that bound the two together. It connected them to the outside world by river and road, and facilitated diplomatic, commercial and military travel. In the process Perth became the wealthiest town north of Berwick-upon-Tweed, and the dues levied on foreign trade were a very important source of royal revenue.

Perth was one of Scotland's first Royal Burghs, its mediaeval capital, and latterly its official Second City. From the early 17th century, when the English term 'City' was first used in Scotland, Perth was consistently referred to as a City, and its chief magistrate as the Lord Provost. In the 19th and the first 75 years of the 20th centuries, it was recognised in official documents as the *City and Royal Burgh of Perth*.

Then in 1975, as part of the reorganisation of Scottish Local Government, all the Royal Burghs were abolished, and Perth lost its City Status and its Lord Provost, and was no longer accorded precedence as the Second City of Scotland.

The people of Perth, however, were in denial. They continued to refer to their home as a City, often the 'Fair City', as it had been called in Sir Walter Scott's novel *The Fair Maid of Perth*. Furthermore, the debilitating effects of the loss of status were slow to materialise. In terms of population and wealth, the other four cities of Scotland – Edinburgh, Glasgow, Aberdeen and Dundee – were in a very different category from Perth, and indeed from every other town in Scotland, and so Government policies targeted on the Big Four were not seen to discriminate against Perth.

That changed in 2000, when Inverness became Scotland's fifth city, and the change was reinforced when Stirling joined the city ranks in 2002. Moreover, the Scottish Executive (later the Scottish Government) gradually began to promote policies, ranging from broadband connectivity to the restoration of historic buildings, specifically for Scotland's cities. This changed emphasis gathered momentum following the Scottish Parliamentary elections in 2007, when the SNP formed its first administration and a Minister for Cities was appointed (Nicola Sturgeon MSP).

After two missed opportunities, in 2007 Perth & Kinross Council decided to apply for City Status in the expected Diamond Jubilee Civic Honours competition. Neither the opportunities which would await a new City of Perth, nor the potential costs of failure, had been foreseen at that time.

The restoration of City Status was to prove to be the most important event in Perth's history since the publication in 1828 of Scott's novel, *The Fair Maid of Perth*. It brought investment and structural renewal to Perth, and a clutch of economic programmes, targeted by the Government at Scotland's cities. Without it, the outlook for the community of Perth would have been bleak.

Perth's success in the City Status competition in 2012 was achieved against enormous odds. But it was not a freak event. It was the culmination of a carefully planned campaign, fought with vigour and enthusiasm by the people of Perth, and supported eventually by the whole nation of Scotland.

The main stages of the campaign were: the Year of the Homecoming throughout 2009; the Westminster Dinner and the first application for City Status in December 2009; the Perth800 campaign in 2010 to mark the 800th anniversary of Perth's King William the Lion Charter; the second application for City Status in May 2011; and the final effort, during the autumn and winter of 2011/12, to catch the attention of those who might influence the result.

At the beginning, when it was assumed that there would be awards for each of the nations of the United Kingdom, the campaign strategy was to promote Perth as the leading contender among the Scottish towns. Then when it was announced that there would be only one award for the whole of the UK, and it became clear that Perth was to be the only Scottish applicant, the campaign was refocussed to marshall the support of the whole nation of Scotland behind Perth's claim.

This is the history of the campaign, of its successful outcome and of the legacy that it bestowed. It finishes with a speculative look into the future for the City of Perth.

CHAPTER ONE

Introduction

Perth's campaign to secure City Status in the Diamond Jubilee Civic Honours competition was beset by unexpected challenges not from the potential competition in Scotland, but from hostility in London. The hostility was not directed at Perth, but at the prospect of even more cities in the UK. And so the first obstacle to overcome was to ensure that there would actually be a competition.

There had been Civic Honours competitions for the Queen's 40th anniversary in 1992 (although no Scottish towns were involved), at the Millennium and for the Golden Jubilee celebrations in 2002. It was confidently assumed, not only in Perth but in several ambitious towns in England as well, that there would be one for her Diamond Jubilee. However, as preparations for the celebrations progressed, it gradually became apparent that a Civic Honours Competition was not part of the official plan.

In fact the whole concept of the competition had to be rescued from death row in Downing Street, where many of Prime Minister Gordon Brown's cabinet were unenthusiastic. They felt that any positive political fallout from the successful town or towns would be far outweighed by the negative backlash from the many unsuccessful candidates. Several also believed that there were too many

cities already, especially around the UK's celtic fringe, where Scotland already had six (Edinburgh, Glasgow, Aberdeen, Dundee, Inverness and Stirling), and Wales and Northern Ireland, five each. Meanwhile, there were 50 cities in England.

When, belatedly, a Civic Honours competition was announced (as a direct result of Perth's intervention), it was made clear that there would be only one winner from the whole of the UK. This stacked the cards even more heavily against the Fair City. What chance would Perth (population 45,000) have against the weight of the expected competition from huge English towns, some with populations more than four times that of Perth? Moreover many of these candidate towns were not far from London, and were well known to politicians of all parties. Their MPs were friends and allies of those who would compile the report and make the recommendation to HM the Queen. Perth, remote, small, unfamiliar and represented by the Scottish National Party (SNP) which was an alien party in Westminster, would be battling against the odds.

In addition to difficulties in London, Perth had problems at home. In the past its attitude to competitions for official city status had been lukewarm and defeatist. Perth had shunned two recent opportunities to compete for city status. The opinion in the Fair City was that Perth was a city anyway, it had always been a city, and everyone knew it was a city. There was no need for any further official recognition. If Perth entered the competition and was unsuccessful, its lowly status as a town would be confirmed, emphasised and broadcast. Better not to try.

Worse, there were influential naysayers in London, in Edinburgh and even within Perth & Kinross Council, who doubted that Perth had ever been a real city, and were scornful of the claim that Perth had been the capital of Scotland for many centuries. Following the General Election in 2010, which brought the Conservative/Liberal Democrat coalition to power, Michael Moore MP, the recently appointed Secretary of State for Scotland, said that he did not believe that there was any real evidence that Perth had ever had 'official' city status. Others in Edinburgh and even in Perth agreed with him. 'There is no documentary evidence of city status', they said, 'No Charter, no Letters Patent, no record of a Royal Declaration'.

As for Perth's claim to have been the capital of Scotland, they pointed out that in mediaeval times the Royal Court was peripatetic, travelling around the country to impress the lieges in as many places as possible. They were unimpressed by evidence that until 1437, Perth was the place to which the King returned following such peregrinations; it was where the Parliament and Church Council were most frequently convened; where major treaties were signed, where the monarchs were crowned and where the Royal Mausoleum was built. Perth it seemed was not even considered to be *primus inter pares*.

Civic morale was low.

However, the mood began to change in 2004. It is difficult to pin down any definite reasons for the change, but perhaps it was because Stirling, for a long time Perth's rival for civic prestige, appeared to have gained significantly from its promotion to City Status in 2002, while Perth languished as a mere town. Councillors may also have noticed the beginning of the change in the way the Scottish Executive (now into its second term) treated Scotland's cities. Increasingly, cities were being seen as the driving force of Scotland's economy, and for that reason were in receipt of special attention and money from the Scottish budget. It began to look as if Perth might lose out.

There was also a change in the Administration of the Council. Since 1999 the SNP had been by far the largest party in the Council, although it was just short of an overall majority, and was unable to persuade any of the other parties, or any of the Independents, to form a partnership. Consequently, a 'Rainbow Coalition' of all the non-SNP councillors (Conservative, Liberal-Democrat, Labour and Independent), had been in power, promoting a programme based on those policies that could be agreed by parties whose fundamentally different philosophies were subordinated to a determination to keep out the SNP at all costs. This continued after the 2003 council elections, but collapsed in the summer of 2004 due to infighting within the coalition. It was replaced by a much more cohesive SNP/Liberal-Democrat partnership with a pro-active approach to local politics.

At that time, preparations for the G8 Summit to be held in Gleneagles Hotel in July 2005 had already begun to involve several Council departments, especially Planning, Transport, Waste Management, the Environment, and the Perth & Kinross sections of Tayside Police and the Tayside Health Board. Senior Councillors and Council officials worked with a range of Scottish and UK government departments and agencies in a period of hectic preparations. In due course, the Summit itself passed off very successfully.

Perthshire, Auchterarder and Perth itself received massive exposure in the world's press and TV networks. It was not just the international officials and their negotiating teams, but also the army of reporters, security staff and journalists from all over the world, and the hordes of protesters, who were exposed to the beauties and delights of Perthshire. In the ten years since the G8, much anecdotal evidence has accumulated of people, from London policemen (who were billeted in the Fishers Hotel in Pitlochry) to middle class protesters, whose first experience of Perthshire was the G8 Summit, but who then returned with their families as tourists.

As the preparations for the G8 developed, the warm congratulations that the Council received for its efficient handling of the many difficult issues encouraged some to believe that Perth might be able to claim City Status in recognition of these efforts, which were as well managed as might have been expected from any large metropolitan authority.

Accordingly, on the 23 March 2005, a Special Council meeting was convened in the historic Old Council Chamber, in front of the press and the TV cameras. A statement reaffirming Perth as a City was read by Provost Bob Scott and signed by all the councillors. The Council then resolved to write to Scottish Ministers asserting Perth's right, as a City, to take its place alongside Scotland's other cities in shaping the nation's future development, and to be given the same status and opportunities by the Scottish Executive. It also resolved to make representations to the UK and Scottish Parliaments, requesting that as an official outcome of the G8 Summit, Perth should be awarded City Status at the conclusion of the Summit in recognition of the Council's efforts in staging the event.

Predictably, the request was refused, although the town of Auchterarder, which had endured much disruption, was (after a long delay) given a grant of £500,000 towards the cost (£1.25m) of restoring its historic Aytoun Hall. The people of Perth, and their representatives, were left to wonder whether the past decisions not to pursue City Status through the Civic Honours competitions had been wise.

Ancient Capital of Scotland

From the very beginning our aim was to differentiate Perth from the other candidate towns by emphasising that we were seeking the **restoration** of the ancient dignity of City Status that had been removed in 1975. And yet we knew that Perth's claims to have been, *de facto*, the capital of Scotland in the mediaeval period, one of Scotland's first Royal Burghs and wealthiest towns, and latterly the official Second City of Scotland, would meet with considerable scepticism.

And so we realised that success in the Civic Honours competition would depend to a great extent on verifying the detail and historical veracity of these claims.

In Scotland, where the word 'city' did not enter general use until around 1600, the most important of the larger settlements were classified as 'royal burghs', and others as 'burghs'. So it is inappropriate to use the term 'capital city' in relation to Scotland during the mediaeval period. However, it was during the latter part of that time, especially the 14th and early 15th centuries, when the concept of a national capital was emerging in Europe, that Perth was Scotland's foremost settlement, and much more important than Edinburgh.

Following the murder of King James I in the Blackfriars monastery

in Perth in 1437, the Royal Court, feeling insecure in Perth, moved to Edinburgh, which in due course became Scotland's official capital. Perth, however, then became Scotland's official 'Second City', a distinction it defended in the highest court of the land from competing claims by Dundee. This lasted until the reorganisation of Local Government in 1975, when all the burghs and royal burghs were abolished, and Perth, uniquely, lost its City Status and Lord Provostship.

An ancient title that was not abolished however, was Perth's Lord Dean of Guild, who presided over the Dean of Guild Court. Perth has perhaps the oldest Guildry Incorporation in Scotland, dating back to the William the Lion Charter of 1210. Its 'Locket Book' is one of the earliest records of Guildry proceedings. The Lord Dean is now a ceremonial appointment, but it was at one time invested with

Among the earliest records of Guild proceedings in Scotland is Perth's 'Locket book'. It contains records of the organisation from 1452, and a number of important royal signatures.

considerable power and influence. Remarkably the office of the Lord Dean survived the attention of the zealots who stripped Perth of its City Status and Lord Provostship, perhaps because they were unaware that it existed.

Scotland before MacAlpin

Mainland Scotland in the early 9th century was roughly divided into three. The Picts controlled the greatest area – the east and north of the country from the modern counties of Fife and Perthshire to Caithness, and the area from Loch Etive and the Sound of Mull northwards, including Skye and the Inner Hebrides. Pictland was divided into seven Provinces, which were constantly vying with each other for supremacy.

The Scots, who had descended from Irish settlers from County Antrim controlled the area from Oban to the Firth of Clyde. The Picts and the Scots were regularly at war with each other. Dominance swayed from east to west and back, and was complicated by regular intermarriage between the royal households.

South of Scotland's central belt were the Angles in *Bernicia*, the modern Lothian and Borders regions, and the Britons in Strathclyde and Dumfries-shire These were the northern elements of powerful kingdoms based in Northumberland and Cumbria.

Scone: 843 to c950

By the middle of the 9th century Scone was the royal centre of an ambitious tribe inhabiting the Pictish

province of Fortriu which comprised the historic County of Perthshire and included the area around Menteith. It had come to dominate the provincial war lords and kinglets of Pictland from the Forth to the Pentland Firth. It had embraced Christianity in the 7th century, when monks from Iona set up a monastery at Scone, and by the 8th century there was also a major Christian centre in Abernethy. It had an important palace at Forteviot as well as defensive

Scotland in the time of Kenneth MacAlpin: Pictland to the north, Dal Riata to the west, and in the south the Britons and the Angles.

The cairn on the top of Moncreiffe Hill overlooking the rivers Tay and Earn.

Below

The volcanic outcrop of Dunadd dominates the surrounding flat marsh land around the River Add.

Right

Moot Hill, topped by the Mansfield mausoleum and surrounded by high trees.

establishments at Moot Hill in Scone, at Dundurn in West Strathearn, and on Moncreiffe Hill.

Then in 843AD, the long running rivalry between the Picts and the Scots was settled when, in a battle near Scone, Kenneth MacAlpin, King of the Scots, defeated Drosten, the last King of the Picts, whose forces

had been weakened by recent Viking raids. MacAlpin subsequently moved his court from Argyll to Scone.

The centre of MacAlpin's kingdom of Dal Riata had been at Dunadd, near Crinan, a rocky outcrop amid the tidal marshes around the River Add. On close examination it is clear that MacAlpin's two royal centres had a great deal in common. If the relatively modern Scone Palace (dating originally, from the 1580s), the Mausoleum and the large trees are swept away, the landscape surrounding Moot Hill can be seen to be very similar to that around Dunadd. It is a relatively small mound, but it stands on top of a significant escarpment about 100 feet above what was a tidal marsh stretching north, west and south to the River Tay. In MacAlpin's time it

would have had a 360-degree view, south to the early settlement at Perth, west across to the Ochil Hills, north up the Tay valley, and east to the Sidlaw Hills. Furthermore, the approach up the slope from the south was protected by the deep gully of the Catmoor burn. MacAlpin could have had no better lookout or defensive position. This strategic location led to its cultural and ceremonial importance. It became the seat of Royal power in Scotland, and the site of the enthronement of Scotland's monarchs for 700 years.

Sadly, the landscape significance of Moot Hill is now greatly diminished. The enormous bulk of Scone Palace was built along the top of the escarpment, completely obscuring the Hill from the River Tay, and so depriving it of its strategic and psychological importance. More recently, large trees have been planted on its slopes, further limiting the outlook and reducing its impact.

MacAlpin brought with him the Gaelic language, which gradually usurped the language of the Picts, which has now been completely lost. He also brought with him the Stone of Destiny and the Irish traditions of enthroning the new king. His immediate task was to establish his dynasty and consolidate his rule over the more distant Pictish provinces, and unite the peoples of the east and west of the country to create the embryonic Kingdom of Scotland, the first Nation State in Europe.

Under MacAlpin's successors, Scone continued to be the Royal

Centre, where the Scots Kings were enthroned by being seated on the Stone of Destiny. The first positive record of such an enthronement was that of King Girie, (a nephew of MacAlpin) in 877 or 878, and it is almost certain that for over four hundred years all the Kings of Scots were enthroned on the Stone of Destiny until it was removed by Edward I of England in 1296. At such an enthronement, the Stone was brought from safe keeping in the Abbey, and placed outside at the east end of the Abbey church, where the ceremony took place. The Stone was

Looking up from the River Tay to Scone Palace which was built along the edge of the escarpment, giving it a magnificent setting and tremendous views, but depriving Moot hill of its landscape significance

Replica of the Stone of Destiny, on Moot Hill, outside Scone Palace

Perth from Woodend, by Alexander Duff Robertson (1807–1886), showing Greyfriars Harbour at the outfall of the southern arm of the Lade. Note Monk's tower, an important element of the city wall.
© Perth & Kinross Council

Gold brooch inlaid with niello, a dark compound of silver.
© Perth & Kinross Council.

not left outside to endure the vicissitudes of the weather, and the ceremonies did not take placed on Moot Hill.

Crowning was an English custom, and was first used in Scotland in 1306 by Robert the Bruce, who was the first king to be inaugurated after the theft of the Stone of Destiny by Edward I of England.

MacAlpin's grandson, Constantine II, who reigned for 40 years from 900AD, extended his

---

1 A.A.M. Duncan: 'Scotland, the Making of the Kingdom, the Edinburgh History of Scotland, Volume One. Oliver & Boyd, 1975, pp 56–58.

authority across the central belt into the Lothians and Strathclyde, the first King of Scots to do so.[1]

Perth in the early mediaeval period

In the first years of the second Millennium, although Scone continued to be the royal and religious centre, a commercial settlement was arising at Perth, at the harbour and around the ford, and later the mediaeval bridge. Perth was at the nodal point of the developing kingdom – the lowest bridging and fording point, and the upper limit of navigation – which ensured its strategic, diplomatic, administrative and commercial importance.

The two centres developed in tandem. From Scone the land routes stretched out to Scotland's east coast; via the Mounth to modern Aberdeenshire and the Moray Firth; and up the Tay valley to the north and north west. From Perth the connections were south east to Edinburgh and Abernethy and south to the palace at Forteviot and the River Earn. This river provided a corridor westwards to the mountain passes leading to Dal Riata and MacAlpin's earlier stronghold at Dunadd. Furthermore, from Perth's harbour, MacAlpin's experienced navigators could reach the more far-flung areas of the developing nation more quickly and safely than by land.

Perth's rich archaeological remains confirm that Perth developed as a trading port in the first and second centuries of the second millennium (see opposite).

Evidence of the close links between Scone and Perth is found in concessions given by King Alexander I to the monastery of Scone. Alexander, who founded the Priory of Scone in around 1120 wished to encourage the new monastery to develop trade with England and to do so he offered a tax free ship to come to the port of Perth. He also encouraged 'all the merchants of

England', by offering to all who wished to trade with his new monastery in Scone, a peaceful passage to Perth.[2]

Around the middle of that period the mediaeval bridge and the castle were built, greatly enhancing Perth's trading and military status. The bridge continued the line of the High Street crossing Stanners Island to the east bank. The castle was built on a mound near where the Museum now stands, and overlooked the outfall of the Lade. A sheriff was installed there in 1150, and from the castle the administration of the fledgling state

---

2 'Perth: The First Hundred Years'. Matthew Hammond: Journal of the Perthshire Society of Natural Science, Vol XIX, 2012, p 63; 'Scotland: The Making of the Kingdom, the Edinburgh History of Scotland, Volume One, Oliver & Boyd, 1975, pp 56–58.

A bronze plaque showing the castle and mediaeval bridge. It can be found on the flood wall adjacent to the large gate at the North Inch.

Bottom

Artist's impression of the appearance of mediaeval Perth from the east bank of the river. The castle on the right is separated from the city by the outfall of the Lade. The city wall runs along the inner bank of the lade, and the bank of the river to the mediaeval bridge. St John's Kirk dominates its surroundings.
© Perth & Kinross Heritage Trust.

The Charter, granted by King William I (The Lion), which conferred Royal Burgh Status on Perth.

Courtesy Perth Museum and Art Gallery.

© Perth & Kinross Council.

indigenous tribes were Angles from Northumberland, rather than Picts or Scots from the North and West.

In mediaeval times – and indeed for many subsequent centuries – roads, where they existed, were primitive and dangerous, and so goods and passengers were carried by ship, whenever possible. In these circumstances, a port 30 miles inland, at the geographic centre of the nation, providing access to all parts of central Scotland, and to the main routes to the North and West, was a huge advantage.

From the harbour at Perth direct and safe trade could be conducted with all the important towns on the east coasts of Scotland and England, and across the North Sea to Scandinavia, the Baltic countries and northern Europe. Harbour dues and other fees made Perth the second wealthiest burgh in Scotland, second that is to Berwick-upon-Tweed, and far wealthier and more important than Edinburgh. As well as trade, wealth and a cosmopolitan population, the harbour brought prestige and influence by enabling the exchange of religious and royal emissaries to and from all parts of Europe.

was conducted. This castle was regularly used by the kings of Scotland until it was swept away in the terrible flood of 1209. Indeed King William I (The Lion) had to be rescued from the castle during that flood. Gratitude to the citizens of Perth for saving his life was one of the reasons for granting Perth its Charter. The castle was not rebuilt.

Even without a castle, Perth was a secure and defensible location for the royal court. It was farther from England than Scotland's other major Royal Burghs (Berwick-upon-Tweed, Roxburgh and Edinburgh) and its whole population could be defended behind its high walls, which were in turn protected by a moat formed by the Town Lade and the river – the only stone walled and moated Royal Burgh in Scotland.

Meanwhile Edinburgh was isolated from the bulk of Scotland by the long arm of the Firth of Forth and the treacherous marshland of the Carse of Stirling. Furthermore, its

Scottish Burghs

Burghs, the third of Scotland's three estates (after the Bishops and the Nobility) were the backbone of urban Scottish life for centuries. Burghs were typically settlements under the protection of a castle or religious establishment, to which taxes were paid. Royal Burghs were created by the King and were generally the largest, wealthiest burghs, and most were ports. Only Royal Burghs could engage in foreign trade, on which custom dues were paid to the king. They enjoyed trading privileges and regulated their own affairs to a greater or lesser extent, depending on the type of burgh. All burghs had internal organisations including magistrates and officers at arms, which ensured order, prosperity and civic pride.

Perth's Lord Provost's badge and double chain are testament to the importance of civic order. The circumstances around their commissioning, and their provenance, are well documented. The hand written Council Minute of March 1791, which authorised the expenditure on badges and chains for the Lord Provost and Bailies states, 'it being particularly necessary when they (the magistrates) are called upon to quell mobs or tumults, that they

have some marks to distinguish them from other inhabitants'. The badge features *Justitia* the Roman goddess of Justice holding the sales of justice in one hand, and a sword in the other. During the Victorian era, other cities and towns in Scotland commissioned much more elaborate badges for their officials, and so Perth may have the oldest Provost's badge in Scotland sill in regular use.

The rights and privileges of the burghs and royal burghs were jealously guarded, and protected in the Act of Union in 1707. They survived thereafter for over two and a half centuries until they were abolished by the reorganisation of Local Government in 1975.

Perth's pre-eminence among Royal Burghs

Sixteen royal burghs were established by King David I (reigned 1124–1153), six in the first three years of his reign – Berwick, Roxburgh, Dunfermline, Edinburgh, Stirling and of course, Perth. None of King David's charters survives, so it is impossible to say if one of them could claim seniority. Of these burghs Berwick was the largest, wealthiest and most important, but is now in England. Roxburgh was razed to the ground, and Dunfermline had by the 14th century become dependent on the Abbey. Of the three remaining burghs, only Perth and Edinburgh were important enough in 1357 to send representatives to the first Scottish parliament to include members from the third estate – the Scottish Burghs

Perth's Lord Provost's badge and double chain.

In 2010, Perth's 800th anniversary celebrations commemorated the granting of a Royal Charter by King William the Lion. This confirmed and expanded the terms of King David's earlier charter of about 1127 conferring Royal Burgh status on Perth. A copy of King William's charter survives and can be seen in the Perth Museum.

In 1960, Perth celebrated the 750th anniversary of King William's charter, which at that time was thought to have been dated in 1210, the year after the flood. By 1975, however, Professor AAM Duncan, the most eminent historian of the period, had come to the opinion that the Charter was probably granted in August 1209, shortly after the flood. Nevertheless, for administrative and other reasons it was decided in Perth to celebrate the 800th anniversary in 2010, rather than 2009.

Treaties

The capital of a nation will normally be the location where important international treaties are negotiated and signed.

This was the case in 1266, when the Treaty of Perth, Scotland's most important international treaty in mediaeval times. was signed in Blackfriars Monastery, by King Alexander III of Scotland and King Magnus VI of Norway. The treaty ended nearly two centuries of Norwegian rule in the Western Isles.

Following the Battle of Largs in 1263, and the subsequent death of the Norwegian King Haakon IV in Orkney, there were three years of armed skirmishing up the west coast of Scotland, while at the same time negotiations between envoys of the two countries were continuing. Eventually a deal was struck which ceded the Hebrides and Isle of Mann to Scotland in return for a down payment of 4,000 merks, and 100 marks annually thereafter.

In the summer of 1266 the Norwegians sailed up the River Tay to Perth, where the King was in residence, and the Treaty was signed on 2 July. Apart from the Northern Isles, the Isle of Man and Berwick-upon-Tweed, Scotland's borders have not changed since.

Next in importance to the Treaty of Perth was the Auld Alliance between Scotland and France, which was signed in Paris in 1295. The genesis of the Auld Alliance was the repeated humiliation of King John Balliol by Edward I of England. The leading Scottish nobles and clergy appointed a group of 12 of their number, the 'Council of Twelve', to take matters out of the hands of the King, and negotiate a treaty of mutual protection with France. When this Alliance was ratified in Scotland, the seals of Scotland's leading nobles and clergy were appended, and those of six important burghs, of which Perth was one.

In 1296, Edward retaliated, and rampaged through Scotland, precipitating the Wars of Independence, further humiliating King John Balliol, who abdicated in July of that year, and carrying off the Honours of Scotland and the Stone of Destiny. Scottish burghs were forced to submit to his rule, each one appointing 12 burgesses to speak on its behalf – except for Perth, which was represented by 18 burgesses, 'presumably because Perth was more important than the others, and its governing group larger'.[3]

A gruesome indication of the strategic military importance of Perth and the Tay crossing during the Wars of Independence, was that following the obscene execution of William Wallace, his head was piked on London Bridge, and the quarters of his dismembered body were displayed in Newcastle, Berwick, Perth and Aberdeen.

Parliament

Between the 13th and 15th centuries parliaments were peripatetic meetings usually in the large religious houses, which were the only places which had appropriate facilities. The first record of a Parliament was in Scone in 1265. Subsequently, Scone Abbey was a favoured location especially during the 1300s, hosting 21 of the 37 Parliaments convened in that century. While the Royal Apartments were in Scone Abbey, safely distant from the crowded streets of Perth, many of the senior clergy and nobles, and certainly their extended retinues would have lodged in Perth.

Around 1400, the Parliamentary focus shifted from Scone Abbey to

Blackfriars Monastery, built outside the city wall adjacent to the North Inch in Perth, where the King was a regular resident. During the first half of that century 14 of the 21 sessions of Parliament were held in Perth, compared with only five in Edinburgh.

For nearly 200 years, therefore, the huge majority of Scottish Parliaments were convened either in Scone or Perth, more than in all the other burghs and royal burghs of Scotland put together. Furthermore, it was during this time that the third estate, the Burghs of Scotland began to be represented in the Scottish Parliaments. The Parliaments of 1357–1367 were the first to list the burghs attending, and, as noted above, Perth was one of them.

A Royal Mausoleum

King James I clearly favoured Perth as his royal centre, for he built a Royal Mausoleum at the Carthusian Monastery, where the King James VI Hospital now stands. No monarch would build a Royal Mausoleum anywhere other than in the capital of his country. James was buried there following his assassination in 1437, as was his Queen, Joan Beaufort in 1445. It continued as an important building in Perth for over 100 years, being used in 1541 for Queen Margaret Tudor, the sister of Henry VIII of England and widow of King James IV, who was killed at Flodden. Sadly, the monastery and mausoleum were completely destroyed in the Reformation and nothing now remains above the ground. The only reminder is the memorial to James I

3 A.A.M. Duncan, *Perth, the First century of the Burgh*, Transactions of the Perthshire Society of Natural Science, 1973, p 46

BLACKFRIARS WYND

Nothing of Blackfriars Monastery remains, save a fragment of wall within the Fair Maid's House. Its location is commemorated in this street name.

Memorial to James I on the site of the Carthusian monastery.

Right

Text on the shaft of the memorial: Within these grounds stood the Carthusian monastery, founded by James 1 of Scotland in 1428. It was the only house belonging to this order in Scotland. In the precincts of the Monastery were buried: The Royal Founder, His Queen Joan Beaufort, and Margaret Tudor, Queen of James IV.

on the corner of King Street and Hospital Street.

The assassination of King James 1 in Blackfriars Monastery in 1437 was a disaster for the centrality of Perth within Scotland, thwarting the process by which it was emerging as the official capital of the country. The Court felt insecure in Perth, and moved to Edinburgh, which was declared the official capital in 1452. The parliamentary emphasis followed, with 44 parliaments convened between 1450 and 1500, all but three of which were held in Edinburgh, and only one in Perth.

National Council of the Scottish Clergy

Throughout this period the Catholic Church was enormously powerful and owned a great deal of property. Its influence permeated every strand of Scottish life, from the Royal Court to the humblest peasant. Prior to 1472, however, there was no

Archbishop at the apex of this establishment, so Scotland was considered to be a 'Special Daughter of the See of Rome', and its affairs were administered by a powerful body called the National Council of the Scottish Clergy. Meetings of this body were held uniformly in Perth until 1459.

Scotland's Second City, and the importance of Precedence

After Edinburgh achieved official capital status in 1452, Perth was granted precedence over all the other burghs and royal burghs, becoming Scotland's official 'Second City', although that term was not used at the time. Precedence was very important, not only for the burghs, but among the nobles and clergy as well, and disputes about it led to fisticuffs (among supporters), legal actions, and even duels.

In the 'Riding of Parliament' at the opening of a Parliamentary session, the Crown and Honours of Scotland were paraded at the head of a procession up the Royal Mile from Holyrood Palace to Parliament Hall. The dignitaries involved left Holyrood Palace in reverse order of precedence, the lowest ranking going first. They processed up the High Street and then waited at the door of Parliament Hall until the King arrived and entered, followed in the proper order of precedence by the nobles, then the clergy and lastly the burgh representatives. Edinburgh was the first of the burghs, followed by Perth and then the other burghs in order.

Between 1567 and 1602, there was a long running, and very bitter, dispute between Dundee and Perth as to which should be second after Edinburgh. The dispute swung back and forward between the Convention of Burghs and the Parliament, and was complicated by a separate issue about control of the Tay estuary. Stirling weighed in with a claim that it should have second place rather than Perth or Dundee, and Linlithgow and Aberdeen each claimed third place after the victor in the dispute for second place.

Eventually, the matter was referred to the Court of Session for a decision, and this took place on the 30 December 1602. It was so important that the King himself was present. The judgement for, 'Precedence in Parliaments, General Conventions, Councils of the Estates of the Realm, and Assemblies of Burghs', was settled in Perth's favour. Although the matter was not seriously challenged thereafter, there were intermittent rumblings of discontent from Dundee, and further legal clarification was required two centuries later, in 1804.

The dispute about the Tay estuary continues to this day. The problem was, and still is, that the commercial viability of Perth's harbour is affected by the charges levied by the Dundee Port Authority on passing ships, including on those that do not dock in Dundee. As recently as 2005, the matter was raised yet again. The occasion was an official visit to Perth by Tavish Scott MSP, the Minister for Transport in the Scottish Parliament, but despite promises to investigate the situation, it remains unresolved.

After the Union of Parliaments in 1707, the General Assembly of the Church of Scotland, which was

Loading timber at Perth Harbour.

Scotland's surrogate parliament for almost 300 years, became the focus of this display of the importance of precedence. Traditionally the opening of the Assembly was attended by senior judges, sheriffs and civil servants and representatives from all of the burghs. By the mid 20th century, the procession of these dignitaries went from the City Chambers on the High Street of Edinburgh to the General Assembly buildings on the Mound. In this procession, the Lord Provost of Edinburgh went first, and the Lord Provost of Perth second, the rest following in official order. This continued until 1975, when all burghs and royal burghs were abolished, and replaced by Regional and District Councils, and then in 1996 by the Unitary Councils. However, precedence still matters – at least to Edinburgh – for at the procession to the opening of the General Assembly, the Lord Provost of Edinburgh is still first, but sadly for Perth, the Lord Provosts and Provosts of the other councils now follow in alphabetic order.

The Opinion of the Lord Lyon

Retrospective acknowledgement of Perth's one time capital status by the Court of the Lord Lyon, came in 1977 on the occasion of the award of a coat of arms to Perth & Kinross District Council. Following the re-organisation of Local Government in 1975, and the creation of the Regional and District Councils,

the Lord Lyon was initially reluctant to allow Perth & Kinross District Council to use the prestigious double headed eagle bearer, which had featured on the coat of arms of the City and Royal Burgh of Perth. The reason stated was that the District Councils, bereft of important responsibilities that had been transferred to the Regions, were not sufficiently powerful to justify heraldic bearers.

This was a perverse judgement because the same powers had been transferred to the Regions from the City Districts of Edinburgh Glasgow, Aberdeen and Dundee which were allowed to keep their heraldic bearers. The people of Perth found that the decision to allow Dundee to retain its heraldic importance particularly unfair because Dundee was similar in terms of population to Perth & Kinross, but much smaller in area. And so, following a campaign by Perth's councillors and officials, the double headed eagle bearer was allowed as a special case, 'to mark the fact that the City of Perth was a former capital of Scotland, and took

precedence over all Scottish burghs except Edinburgh'.[4]

Surprisingly, the double headed eagle in the 1977 version is black, not golden, but with a red beak and feet. No explanation has been forthcoming for this change. It may be that the Lord Lyon inadvertently chose black, which is the usual colour for such eagle bearers in European heraldry. It appears that the councillors and officials in Perth were so relieved to get back their eagle, that they did not quibble about its colour!

Following the abolition of the Regions and Districts and the creation of Perth & Kinross Unitary authority in 1996, only minimal changes were made to the coat of arms. The coronet encircling the necks of the eagles now has eight spikes alternating with eight thistles, instead of the District Council's eight thistles. (Of course only half of them are visible). In heraldic terms, the spikes are appropriate for an Area Council. The three former (pre-1975) councils each contributes a distinctive

element to the coat of arms. King William's rampant lion holding a scimitar comes from the old Perth County Council, the shield depicting a castle on an island (Loch Leven Castle) comes from Kinross County Council, and the double headed eagle from the old City and Royal Burgh of Perth.

Conclusion

And so, notwithstanding the peripatetic nature of the mediaeval monarchy and parliaments, Perth was pre-eminent among Scottish Royal Burghs. It was close to Scone, where all the kings were inaugurated and it was the centre to which the king returned. It was the location for the majority of parliaments. It was the hub of the Kingdom, not only for travel within Scotland, but also for international travel. It was Scotland's most wealthy burgh, its administrative centre, and increasingly the focus of

---

4   R. M. Urquhart, 'Scottish Civic Heraldry, Published by *Heraldry Today*, 1979, p. 37.

royal activity. It was even the location of the Royal Mausoleum.

No other burgh or royal burgh came near to possessing all these attributes. Edinburgh was not on the coast, nor on a river, and was isolated from the rest of Scotland by the Firth of Forth. Its population, during the MacAlpin dynasty had a different ethnic mix, being part of the Northumbrian clan of Angles, speaking a different language. Stirling was on the border between the Picts and the Britons of Strathclyde, and so on the periphery of the influence of the early kings based in Scone. Both these burghs had defensible castles, but lacked Perth's hub location and access to the sea, and the wealth that flowed from foreign trade.

And so, although the concept of an official 'capital' did not crystallise until later in the 15th century, Perth was the Royal Burgh where, for 600 years, the functions of the national capital of a developing mediaeval European nation took place. When eventually Edinburgh was declared the official capital of Scotland, the Royal Burgh of Perth was given a consolation prize. It became officially the Second City of the nation, with precedence over all the other burghs and royal burghs, a dignity that it enjoyed until 1975. Finally, its earlier status as the former capital of Scotland was eventually acknowledged by the Lord Lyon.

CHAPTER THREE

History of City Status in the United Kingdom

Some of the confusion about Perth's right to claim city status arose from a failure to understand that the Scottish concept of a city was quite different from that in England. The term 'City' was an English word which, prior to 1600 and the Union of the Crowns, had little currency in Scotland, where the legal definition of a settlement outside the feudal system was, as we have seen, either a burgh or royal burgh.

British Cities from the Mediaeval Period until 1900

In the early Middle Ages England had 28 cities, which had developed from strategic Roman fortified towns. The first change took place in the 1540s during the English Reformation when Henry VIII established (by Letters Patent) six new cities, each the centre of a new Church of England diocese, with a bishop and a cathedral. Thereafter the presence of a cathedral was considered to be one of the unstated criteria (in England) for city status. However, no further English cities were created for the next three centuries.

At this time there were no cities in Scotland with any official recognition.

In the second half of the 19th century, following the Industrial Revolution and rapid urbanisation in England, a number of new cities were created by Queen Victoria. Each of these followed the establishment of a new diocese by the Anglican church, and therefore the elevation of the main parish church to a cathedral. As part of this process, Dundee successfully applied for City Status in 1889 – the first city to be created in Scotland by Letters Patent or Royal Charter. In 1891, the boundaries of Aberdeen were enlarged by a Local Act of Parliament, and the opportunity was taken to confirm its city status officially. Inverness applied for city status in 1897, as part of Queen Victoria's Jubilee celebrations, but was refused.

Although that left Perth, Edinburgh and Glasgow without any official recognition of City Status, the continuing use of the title was permitted on account of 'ancient usage'. Increasingly, however, the title came to be applied indiscriminately, without any legal consequences, to several of Scotland's ancient Royal Burghs, and sometimes, confusingly, to some smaller places where there was a cathedral, as in the case of Brechin.

However, there were no further grants of City Status in Scotland until the year 2000.

English, Irish and Welsh cities from 1900–2000

During the first decade of the 20th century there were applications for city status from several English boroughs, which had expanded rapidly during the industrial revolution, all of which were refused. The exception was Cardiff which was successful in 1905 as the 'Metropolis of Wales'. In 1907 King Edward VII established three criteria, although they were not made public at the time. These were that the population should be over 300,000, that the borough should have a 'local metropolitan character' and a record of good local government. Stoke-on-Trent, Portsmouth, Salford, Leicester and Lancaster were all successful before the Second World War.

The experiences of Leicester and Lancaster are relevant to Perth. Leicester was visited by the King in 1919 and elevated to a city on account of its contribution to the war effort, and to 'restore a dignity lost in the past'. This relates to the fact that although Leicester had been an important Roman fortified town, it had not, like most other similar Roman towns, developed into a city during the Middle Ages. Lancaster, although it fell short of the population quota, was elevated because of its 'long association with the crown' and because it was 'the county town of the King's Duchy of Lancaster'.

Following the Second World War, the stream of petitions for City Status in England gathered pace, but in the half century leading up to the Millennium only four boroughs in England were successful: Cambridge, Southampton, Derby and Sunderland.

Of these, Cambridge set an important precedent for Perth. In 1951 it celebrated the 750th anniversary of its first Charter of Incorporation, and used the occasion to mount a successful petition for City Status. In Wales, Swansea

St Patrick's Roman Catholic Cathedral. Armagh.
Image courtesy of Armagh Parish.

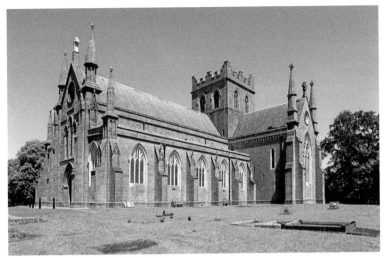

capitalised on the Investiture of the Prince of Wales to mount a successful campaign for City Status in 1969.

The experience of Armagh in Northern Ireland and St David's in Wales, both of which became cities in 1994, demonstrates that population is not so important, and that cathedrals do matter. Armagh was one of the royal capitals of pre-Christian Gaelic Ireland. Then during the Middle Ages it became the ecclesiastical capital of All Ireland and, after the Reformation, the seat of two Archbishops, the Primates of All Ireland for both the Roman Catholic Church and the Anglican Church of Ireland. And of course, it has two cathedrals, both of which bear the name of St Patrick. Nevertheless, its population is less than 15,000.

St Davids is even smaller, with fewer than 2,000 inhabitants, although its cathedral is huge. It is however the final resting place of the Patron Saint of Wales, and is the ecclesiastical capital of the country. Moreover, it was a city in the early Victorian era, but lost that status in 1888.

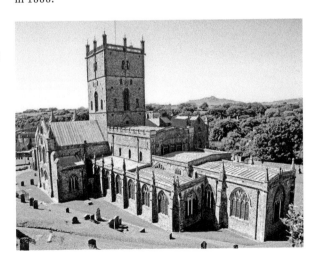

Scottish Cities 'by ancient usage'

It is clear from the above summary that for Perth, Edinburgh and Glasgow, the title *City* was accepted 'by ancient usage'. For Perth and Edinburgh, the lineage of that 'ancient usage' extended back for nearly 900 years, and for Glasgow, which only became a Royal Burgh in 1611, for nearly 400 years. The fundamental point is that in the matter of qualification for City Status, Perth is not different from Edinburgh or Glasgow.

Nevertheless the substantial number of Royal Charters, elevating towns to City Status across the United Kingdom led to doubts about the use of the title *City* by those burghs which had no such documentation. This was particularly the case with Perth, because Edinburgh as the capital of Scotland, and Glasgow as much the largest conurbation, were clearly cities by other definitions.

History of Perth's city status

The Latin language has two words for 'city': *Urbs*, referring to the bricks and mortar of the place, and *civitas* (origin of the word 'city') which referred, according to Cicero, to the social body of its citizens (*cives*) united by the law. The unambiguous description of Perth as a 'City' in an important legal document occurs for the first time in the Charter granted to Perth by King James VI in 1600.

This document, referred to locally as the 'Golden Charter' and written in Latin, consolidated all the previous Royal Charters relating to Perth, and brought them up to date. In it, both of the Latin words for 'city' are used and conjoined in a single sentence with the Latin version of the Scottish word 'burgh'.

> ... having consideration of the ancient erection of our Perth City or our Burgh of Perth [*urbis nostrae Perthensis sue burgi nostri de Perth*] by our renowned predecessors, the Kings of Scots of most worthy memory, into a free city and a regal and royal burgh [*liberam civitatem liberumque regime ac regale burgum*]...

The Golden Charter leaves no room for doubt. Whichever definition is used, and whichever term is applied, Perth was considered by James VI to be a City *and* a Royal Burgh.

The durability of the term 'City of Perth' is borne out almost two centuries later In the *Statistical Account of Perth, 1796*, which notes:

> Perth was long reckoned to be the capital city of Scotland, and now holds priority next to Edinburgh. In several public writs, especially in the time of James VI, it is called the City of Perth, and still bears that title.

From the early 19th century the title *The City and Royal Burgh of Perth* was regularly used in official documents, Acts of Parliament and by-laws approved by the Secretary of State for Scotland. Furthermore, the chief magistrate was referred to as the 'Lord Provost', rather than just the 'Provost' (see Chapter 12). As noted earlier, the epithet 'The Fair City' became widespread following the publication of Sir Walter Scott's novel, *The Fair Maid of Perth* in 1828.

Civic Honours competitions

There was a low key Civic Honours competition in 1992 for HM the Queen's 40th anniversary in which Sunderland was successful, but no Scottish town was involved. The concept of a competition really took off at the Millennium and was promoted strongly by the Westminster Government. In Scotland, Ayr, Paisley, Stirling and Inverness submitted claims, and Inverness was successful. In 2002, on the occasion of HM the Queen's Golden Jubilee, another competition was strongly promoted. On this occasion, Ayr, Paisley, Dumfries and Stirling submitted entries, and Stirling emerged the winner. There was considerable excitement in Inverness and Stirling when the results were announced, and there were early signs that City Status would bring some tangible economic advantages, not available to places like Perth which, whatever their history, had no official recognition.

'Ancient usage' was no longer an adequate substitute in circumstances where several towns in Scotland had submitted unsuccessful City Status competition entries.

Cathedrals and cities in Scotland

The presence of a cathedral with its bishop and associated clergy brought wealth and influence to mediaeval towns. In England most cathedrals were situated in major conurbations. In Scotland however, of at least fourteen cathedrals (not all of which flourished at the same time), only those in Glasgow and Aberdeen were sited in Scotland's main cities.

After the Reformation, St Giles in Edinburgh was the seat of a bishop for two relatively short periods at the time of Restoration of the Episcopacy under Charles I (1635–1638 and 1661–1689). During that time it was correctly styled a cathedral, being the seat of a bishop, and the title has persisted ever since. Nevertheless its

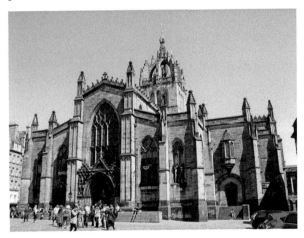

St Giles Cathedral, Edinburgh.

official status, like that of St Machar's and Glasgow cathedrals, and indeed all of the pre-reformation cathedrals that are still in use as churches, is that of a Parish Church of the Church of Scotland. In this respect it should be noted that the Church of Scotland is a thoroughly egalitarian organisation, and all of its parishes have equal status.

St John's Kirk of Perth was never the seat of a bishop, and therefore never a cathedral. It was built as a traditional Scottish 'Burgh Church'

in a much less flamboyant style than Glasgow or St Giles cathedral. It lacked an ambitious bishop with the enormous wealth of the church behind him, who would have created the soaring architecture of a European-style cathedral.

Perth had to rely on royal patronage, and in general the Scottish kings had other more pressing priorities than elaborate church architecture. Nevertheless several of them contributed substantially to St John's. Under these circumstances royal tombs might have been expected in St John's. However, it was not to be. The heart of Alexander III was buried in St John's after his untimely death in 1286, which precipitated the Wars of Independence, but its location is not marked. Robert the Bruce funded the repair of the damage to the Kirk caused by that conflict, but he is buried in Dunfermline Abbey. Robert III gave the citizens of Perth the land comprising the North and South Inches in exchange for the right to be

buried in St John's Kirk. (He is said to have exchanged two inches for six feet!). However the deal was not honoured after his death, and he was buried in Paisley Abbey.

James I was, perhaps, the most Perth-centric of Scotland's monarchs and built his Royal Mausoleum in Perth at the Carthusian monastery, where he was buried after his assassination. Sadly, the monastery and mausoleum were completely destroyed during the Reformation, and nothing now remains above ground. There is, however, the tantalising possibility that a large weathered slab of Tournai marble, mounted vertically against the east wall of St John's Kirk and now partly obscured by a glass wall, is the grave slab of James I and Joan Beaufort, his Queen. The slab would have had brass effigies fixed to it, but now only the outline and lead fixing points remain. The tradition is that during the turmoil of the Reformation, the Carthusian monks rescued the slab, and later it was erected in St John's. Experts, however, doubt the veracity of this tale. They agree that the slab was made for an aristocrat, but believe it may have been for a member of the Mercer family, who had burial rights in St John's Kirk and whose funeral hatchment is fixed the north wall of the north transept.

Top left

Close up of the top of the monument showing King James's monogram 'JR' for 'James Rex', and the date of his assassination 1437. Below is the rampant lion of Scotland. (See p. 24)

Top right

Mercer funeral hatchment in St John's Kirk.

Left

The marble slab on the east wall of St John's Kirk.

St Ninian's cathedral, Perth

The Bishop's Throne in St Ninian's Cathedral.

Eventually when the Episcopalian dioceses of St Andrews, Dunkeld and Dunblane were brought together and established in Perth, a bishop was appointed, and St Ninian's cathedral was built and consecrated in 1850. So far as Perth's Roman Catholic population is concerned, spiritual oversight is exercised by the Bishop of Dunkeld who is based in Dundee.

CHAPTER FOUR

Developing the Strategy

In 2005, after the rejection of Perth's first attempt to win City Status in the wake of the G8 Summit at Gleneagles, there were two years for reflection on what might have been if Perth had entered (and been successful in) one of the two recent Civic Honours competitions. Increasingly, governments in Scotland and elsewhere viewed cities as vital drivers for the whole national economy, so Inverness and Stirling, along with Edinburgh, Glasgow, Aberdeen and Dundee, were included in policies designed to promote cities and develop them as important economic hubs. One such promotion, which was particularly galling for Perth, will serve as an example. It was the business tourism initiative, promoted by VisitScotland, which sought to tap into the booming UK and international conference market. Perth's new concert hall, which opened in 2005, had been designed to accommodate just such events but was excluded from the VisitScotland publicity because it was an exclusive initiative for Scotland's Six Cities. Perth was not a real city.

The Council election of 2007 confirmed the existing SNP/Liberal Democrat partnership in office with a substantial majority. The first Council Meeting after an election is always taken up with the appointment of the Provost, the Leader of the Council, and the Conveners of the committees overseeing the major Council departments. I was hugely privileged to be elected Provost by a unanimous vote, and delighted that my friend and colleague, Ian Miller, was elected the Council leader. We had worked well together in the past and I anticipated a productive working relationship in the future.

Civic Strategy

Even before the new administration was legally constituted, a plan had been conceived to pave the way for a

The spectacular opening of the Concert Hall in 2005, with blue laser lights piercing the sky.
© Graeme Hart

bid for City Status in the civic honours competition which was expected to feature in the Queen's Jubilee celebrations in 2012. I referred to this in my first press interview immediately after my election as provost.

Central to the strategy was the determination that the campaign would be high profile, confident and led by the Provost, that the possibility of failure would not be considered, and that every level of the Council and every section of the Perth & Kinross community would be involved.

In due course the plan was developed by the Council's various committees. In brief the Council decided to embrace the Scottish Government's decision to celebrate 2009 as the *Year of Homecoming*, when the huge Scottish Diaspora across the world (said to number 40 million) would be invited to pay a visit to their homeland to honour the 250th anniversary of the birth of Robert Burns.

Logo for Homecoming 2009.

In Perth, the Year of Homecoming would lead seamlessly to *Perth800*, as the programme of celebrations in 2010 was to be called. This would provide the foundation for our claim for the restoration of City Status. This chimed well with Perth's existing strategy of promoting tourism through events of all kinds, from conferences to sporting competitions, from military parades to museum exhibitions and from business receptions to Royal visits.

The Perth800 programme had three core themes: The Economy, Heritage and Culture & Sport, and three subsidiary topics: Perth's Future, Communities, and Twinning. Every event in the programme was expected to address one or more of these themes and topics. With a lot of public money at stake, there was a need to have an objective assessment of the success or otherwise of the programme. The main economic target was an increase in tourism revenues in Perth City from £77m in 2007 to £83m in 2010. There were three other targets, the RBS UK Affordable Affluence ranking, the Retail Destination Placing, and the Cittaslow Index, all of which were abandoned by their promoters during the aftermath of the banking crash of 2008.

The plan was to enhance existing regular events and establish new ones. These would be developed over the five year period to 2012 and, wherever possible, given an international flavour. During the Year of the Homecoming, over 40 events were staged in Perth & Kinross which attracted recognition as part of the Government's official nationwide programme. This was more than any other local authority other than Edinburgh, Glasgow and Highland. In many cases these were 'dress rehearsals' for even bigger events planned for the Perth800 programme.

In addition, local clubs and societies which were branches of national or international organisations, were encouraged to invite their parent bodies to hold important meetings in Perth. This was remarkably successful, and over the next few years many national and several international societies and clubs held official meetings (AGMs, conferences, etc) in Perth, as guests of their local branches. The Rotary was particularly successful in this respect, with several Districts of Rotary International coming to Perthshire for their annual congresses. In this way we were able to bring to Perth influential business, civic, military, and political individuals, and indeed Royalty. We took great care to point out Perth's strengths to these visitors, alert them to Perth's aspirations, and seek their support for our claim.

For Perth800 the Council staged a number of civic events at strategic intervals throughout 2010 in order to give a framework to the programme, and maintain the momentum. The spaces in between were filled up with a huge variety of events, all promoted under the Perth800 banner. Although City Status was separate from Perth800, it was a persistent strand throughout the campaign. Most of the celebrations were held in Perth, but several, including some very large events took place in locations out-with the city.

The Council allocated £300,000 from its reserves in order to support the Year of Homecoming, Perth800 programmes and the preparation for the City Status bid. Furthermore, organisers of individual events could apply to the Scottish Government (in its various manifestations) for further financial support.

In order to spread the 'ownership' of Perth800 and the City Status bid, representatives of Perth's civic organisations, its clubs and societies and the private sector were included in a broad planning committee which developed the programme. While City Status affected only Perth, the centrality of Perth to the whole region was reflected in the enthusiasm for the project across all of Perth & Kinross.

A separate strand to the strategy was to incorporate into the programme other serendipitous events, in particular military reunions and parades, the granting of full University Status to Perth College UHI by the Privy Council and the relocation of the Head Quarters of the Royal Scottish Geographical Society from Glasgow to Perth, and use them to emphasise Perth's ambition in the wider Scottish context.

Branding

The Council was aware of the importance of branding in the modern communications industry. The Year of the Homecoming had an

The well known cogged wheel logo of Rotary International.

University of the Highlands and Islands Perth College

The fulfilment of a long held dream – Perth was a University City at last.

Royal Scottish Geographical Society

The logo of the RSGS.

Miniature of Tullibardine single malt whisky.

The Perth800 logo.

Small jars of Perthshire heather honey, from Scarlett's apiary in Meigle.

official logo, which could be used to publicise events that had been approved by the Homecoming organisation (see p. 38). The Council's own emblem, featuring its coat of arms, is an historic, colourful, dignified and widely recognised logo, and was authorised for use for all events accepted onto the official programme (see p. 27). However, something special and appropriate for Perth800 was needed. The requirements were that it had to be simple; it had to be recognisably 'Perth', and it had to exude confidence. The eventual design was a masterpiece. It featured a symbolic multi-arched bridge on which was a crown, or a cheering crowd, depending on which way you looked at it. Beneath the bridge are the words **Perth800**, and beneath that, a strap line (in blue to symbolise the river) with the dates **1210–2010**. The logo was easy to reproduce on headed notepaper and programmes etc, and simple enough to be recognisable even when reproduced on a small enamel badge.

The design has stood the test of time and was reproduced the following year when the strap line became **'The Fair City'**, and later still after the success of the City Status

campaign in 2012, it became a victorious **'City of Perth'**, and it is still in use.

As far as possible we sought to emphasise the good things that came out of Perth and Perthshire. And so at official dinners each guest would get a miniature of 12-year-old single malt whisky from the independent Perthshire distiller at Tullibardine[1], and a small jar of Perthshire heather honey from Scarlett's apiary in Meigle. The Council's Design Department did all the artwork for

---

1 The Tullibardine distillery has since been sold to a French wine company.

the labels and produced appropriate bags so that guests left with a good impression of Perth and Perthshire.

The overall objective was to create a positive atmosphere leading to a momentum which would raise the profile of Perth within Scotland and further afield. At that time we expected that there would be a Civic Honours prize for each of the nations of the UK, and that Perth's main competitors would probably be Paisley, Dumfries, Ayr and Dunfermline. We wanted Perth to be seen in Scotland, London, and overseas, as the leading Scottish contender.

Major themes in the City Status campaign

Culture and Sport

Pervading the whole of the Homecoming in 2009, Perth800 and the City Status programmes was an emphasis on culture and sport in the broadest senses. Music and drama, art, architecture and literature, have always been prominent in Perth, and received much financial and moral support from the Council and from local and national trusts and businesses.

The Concert Hall, Perth Theatre, the Museum & Art Gallery, the Fergusson Gallery, St John's Kirk and St Ninian's Cathedral provided the main venues for the cultural programme. In sport, Perth's wealth of provision, from golf courses and bowling greens to curling rinks, an athletics track and indoor facilities at Bell's Sports Centre facilitated a host of national and international competitions.

Goody Bags' appropriately designed.

Below left
High Street entrance to the listed Perth Theatre.

Below right
The entrance to the Bells Sports Centre.

Outward looking focus

Throughout the campaign the Council supported events which emphasised Perth's royal connections, its military links, its national ambition and its European and wider international outlook. Some of the events were fortuitous, especially those involving the military. Perth did not anticipate or plan for the various

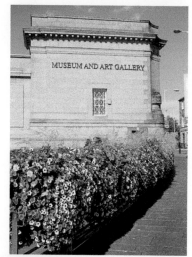

A 'hedge' of wild flowers along the railing between the museum and the Concert Hall.

Perth's continental Café culture in full swing in St John's Place.

re-unions and homecoming parades, but when they were proposed, they were built into our programme as major events.

The desire to promote Perth as a small, but vibrant international city had been evident since its participation in the *Bloom Competitions* in the 1980s and the local planning decisions during the 1990s which sought to promote a European style café culture in the centre of Perth. It was revived by the application to join Cittaslow in 2003 and gathered momentum in 2009 with the Education Department's promotion of a Global Conference and the decision to take part in the competition for the Europe Prize. At the same time, links with our twin cities in Germany, France, Poland, Russia, China and Canada received renewed attention.

Perth in Bloom. Sir Walter Scott was the first to refer to Perth as the 'Fair City' in the novel *The Fair Maid of Perth*. Since then Perth has taken possession of the title, and indeed used it as a surrogate from 1975 to 2012, when official city status was denied. Bloom competitions are judged on Horticultural excellence, Environmental Responsibility and Community Participation. Taking part in these competitions has played a major part in developing and sustaining Perth's reputation as the 'Fair City', and promoting its image not only in Scotland but in England, Europe and even North America. In this, Perth has been ably assisted by towns and villages right across the

The heather garden which includes a National Collection of Heathers in Bellwood Park, beside the stream running down from St Mary's Monastery.

Hanging baskets are an important element of street decoration in Perth.

Council area to such an extent that in 2010, in the Scottish Bloom awards, communities in Perth & Kinross (including Perth itself) collected five major awards. Perth & Kinross was the only Local Authority area to gain more than two awards.

Cittaslow. Cittaslow, meaning 'slow city' in Italian (and pronounced *cheat-a-slow*), is an organisation of small to medium sized towns (under 50,000 population), which started in northern Italy in the 1980s. It seeks to improve the environment and quality of life by reducing pollution and litter, minimising food miles, supporting local agriculture, businesses, public transport and community enterprises, and generally slowing the pace of life.

Towns are assessed against more than 60 criteria and principles which are tangible benchmarks of the quality of life, such as the availability of locally sourced food, support for local shops and businesses, energy conservation, waste management etc. A successful town will have achieved good scores in all of these categories, and to ensure regular renewal of membership must demonstrate that it is striving for continuous improvement. The concept was seen by the Council as an extension of the trajectory established by its success in the *Bloom* competitions, and the establishment of the Farmers' Market. Perth applied in 2003 and gained accreditation in March 2007, the first town in Scotland to do so.

In 2016, there were 147 Cittaslow towns in 74 countries worldwide, of which five (Aylsham, Berwick-upon-Tweed, Llangollen, Mold, and of course Perth) are in the UK.

Cittaslow Supporters. A place with a population of over 50,000 is not eligible to be a Cittaslow town but

cittaslow perth

The snail with a town on its back - the Logo for Cittaslow.

can become a Cittaslow supporter. The goals and criteria are similar to those for Cittaslow towns. The Council area of Perth and Kinross is the UK's first, and so far (2016) the only Cittaslow Supporter.

The Global Conference held in the Concert Hall, in May 2009, explored the importance of global links for educational, cultural and economic development in Perth & Kinross. The speakers included: Alyn Smith MEP – the most internationally experienced of all of Scotland's MEPs; Dr Peter Hughes – the Chief Executive of Scottish Engineering; Carol Craig – Chief Executive of the Centre for Confidence and Well-being, and the author of *The Scots Crisis of Confidence*, a widely praised critique of the Scots psyche; Klaus Herzog – the Oberburgermeister

(Lord Mayor) of Aschaffenburg, Perth's twin city in Germany; and John Fyffe – the Council's Head of Education and Children's Services. The focus was on enterprise and learning. Following the keynote speeches, delegates were able to participate in seminars led by participants from the Scottish Government, the British Council and major Perth businesses. Some more light-hearted entertainment was also provided in the form of music and dance performances by pupils from Perth Academy and Letham Primary School. The event was well attended and widely praised in the media.

The Europe Prize was founded by the Parliamentary Assembly of the Council of Europe in 1955. This organisation, now of 47 member states, was set up by the Treaty of London in 1949 to foster European cooperation and to promote human rights, democracy and the rule of law. It is quite separate from the European Union. Towns and cities competing for the Europe Prize must demonstrate their focus on the European Ideal. There are four stages to the Prize, which must be taken in order: The Diploma, The Flag of Honour; The

Lifting the Tarpaulin, painting by the late artist Michael Scott, on the front cover for the latest edition of Carol Craig's book: *The Scots' Crisis of Confidence*.
Courtesy Michael Scott's widow.

Presentation of the Flag of Honour, the second stage of the Europe Prize to Provost John Hulbert by Professor Miljenko Doric, a senior MP from Croatia, and a member of the Council of Europe.
© Angus Findlay

Plaque of Honour, and The Prize itself. Perth signalled its intention to enter the competition in 2009, and achieved the European Diploma in 2010 and the Flag of Honour in 2011. It was blazing a European trail with these awards. Since the competition was set up, there had been very few award winners from the UK, and no others from Scotland since 1995.

Perth's Twinning Links

Germany This was established in 1956 when, as part of the rapprochement with Germany after the Second World War, Scotland's main cities were each twinned with a city in Bavaria. Perth's twin is Aschaffenburg on the River Maine in the north of the state. This link has proved to be very strong, with many official and unofficial exchanges developing over the years. The 50th anniversary of the twinning was celebrated in a sculpture unveiled on the bank of the River Main in 2006. It consists of two interlocking blocks of sandstone – red for Aschaffenburg and grey for Perth.

As this book goes to press in 2016, there are major celebrations taking place to mark the 60th anniversary of the twinning.

France A different style of relationship was established in 1991 with the town of Cognac in the Charente region of France, based on a shared involvement in distilling. Although all the major cognac distilleries are now owned by multi-national companies, because Cognac must be made from wine sourced from the *Terroire* surrounding the city of that name, *and* be distilled locally, the town has retained a huge distilling industry, similar to Perth's involvement with whisky in the first half of the 20th century. Moreover, many of the ancillary industries, such as a huge bottle making factory are also located in Cognac.

Russia The link with the ancient city of Pskov, in the north west of Russia, was also established in December 1990. It was initiated as a result of a

Former Perth Provost, Bob Scott, and Oberburgermeister Klaus Herzog of Aschaffenburg at the unveiling of the Twinning Stone on the riverside walk called Perth Inch on the banks of the River Main.

While most of the distilling of Cognac is done on a massive scale by multi-national companies, there are still several small (legal) stills on the farmsteads of family owned vineyards.

The Twinning memorial stone in the Riverside Park in Pskov. With me are Cllr Sandy Miller, Tatiana (our guide) and the Lady Provost. The names 'Perth' and 'Pskov' are engraved in Russian and English. 1990 was the year that the agreement was signed in Russia. It was signed in Scotland in 1991.

collaborative theatre production of the musical *Peace Child*, by David Woolcombe, which sought to encourage a resolution to the conflicts between the USA and the USSR by bringing the youth of both countries into contact. Sixteen girls and boys from Pskov were among 140 young people from 14 countries who came together for the musical in Perth, which sold out nine performances. It was a major factor leading to Perth winning the Royal

Blacksmith By 17 year old Nikolai Dementeva, from Pskov.

Courtesy Mr Sandy Miller

Dr Stanislaw Gebertt

Dr Gebertt was a student in Warsaw at the outbreak of the Second World War, and took part in the defence of Warsaw. He was captured by the Russians and sent to a hard labour camp. When Germany invaded Russia in 1941 he escaped, and joined the Polish Army. After campaigns in the Middle East he was sent to Scotland where he trained in the parachute and commando units. In 1943 he was transferred to the Polish Medical Corps, and completed his medical studies in the Polish Medical School in Edinburgh University (See p. 124), graduating in 1947. All his family had lost their lives during the German occupation of Poland, and so he stayed in Scotland.

He specialised in ophthalmology, and worked in Perth Royal Infirmary, and Bridge of Earn Hospital. For many years during the Soviet occupation of his country he was involved with Medical Help to Poland. He visited Bydgoszcz several times, co-ordinating medical aid to the ophthalmology services there. He was awarded the Gold Cross of Merit, and the Cross of Independent Poland by the Polish President. He died in Perth in 2001, and was buried in the Polish military cemetery.

Mail International Twin Town award in 1991.

Since then the Pskov twinning has acquired a momentum of its own, mainly based on art and literature. Visiting groups from both sides regularly negotiate the difficult diplomatic situation to maintain the link. In 2014 the Perth *Friends of Pskov* group arranged for the Pskov

Schools Art Exhibition to be brought to Perth. It included several works of great quality.

Poland Bydgoszcz, a city in central Poland, was twinned with Perth because of the efforts of a Polish ophthalmologist, Dr Gebertt. However, Scotland has long had a special relationship with Poland stretching back many centuries, with substantial population flows in both directions. During the 16th and 17th centuries so many Scots emigrated to Poland that they established Scots Quarters in many of the towns – such as *Das Schottland* (The Scotland District) in Gdansk. The bronze plaque on the wall of the Old Council Chamber testifies to the warm welcome they received.

After the War ended and the Iron

The Polish war memorial overlooks more than 300 Polish military graves in Jeanfield cemetery in Perth.

Curtain descended, many Polish ex-servicemen elected to stay in Scotland, particularly in Perth. The fact that Perth has the largest cemetery for Polish ex-servicemen, with over 300 graves, has contributed to Perth's centrality to the Scottish Polish community. An annual Remembrance service is held each year in front of Perth's striking Polish war memorial. It is attended by the Polish Consul General and senior Polish officials, along with Perth's Provost, councillors, parliamentarians and civic leaders. It is followed by a Mass said in Polish in the Roman Catholic church in Melville Street.

Since Poland joined the EU, the population flow has been from Poland to Scotland, strengthening the links between the two countries. Locally the influx of new arrivals, who are contributing strongly to the economy, has refreshed the local Polish community and revitalised the

Plaque outside the Old Council Chambers at 3 High Street, recording the appreciation of the Polish soldiers for their welcome in Perth.

Mr Konstanty Dombrowicz, the President (Lord Mayor) of Bydgoszcz gives the Fair Maid of Perth a hug during an official visit to Perth.
© Angus Findlay

twinning link between Perth and the City of Bydgoszcz.

Canada Perth also has a strong twinning link with the town of Perth, in Ontario, Canada. The town was originally colonised by emigrants mainly from Perthshire, many of whom were stone masons engaged on the building of the Rideau Canal which connects Ottawa and Kingston on Lake Ontario. The local stone is limestone, which has been used in the construction of many of its fine

The 'Town Crier' has an important official position in many Canadian towns. Here Perth's Town Crier makes an official announcement.

A different 'Perth in Bloom'. River View Café by the River Tay in Perth, Ontario.

buildings. The town sits on both sides of a much smaller and more docile River Tay.

In 2016, Perth, Ontario commemorated the 200th anniversary of its foundation, with a delegation from Perth, Scotland, at the event.

China There is also an official twinning link with the city of Haikou in southern China. Haikou has a population measured in millions which makes meaningful relationships quite difficult. Nevertheless, as Provost, I was invited to lead a delegation from Perth & Kinross Council and Perth College UHI to Haikou.

The reception we received was lavish, with spectacular entertainment and formal dinners from the city authorities, and also from the University of Haikou. We were able to develop the already important links between the University and the English Language and the Hospitality departments in Perth College, and the Golf Management course (which is based in the North Highland College at Dornoch).

We also visited the No 1 Middle School which is linked to Perth High School. Here, the élite of Haikou, 7,000 16- and 17-year-olds, live in the school during the week, and are educated to a very high standard. We got the impression that the discipline was strict, but the children compliant and industrious.

Australia Perth also has an official 'Friendship Agreement' with the city

of Perth in Western Australia. As with the link with Haikou, this is hampered by the huge disparity in size and wealth between Perth WA and Perth Scotland. Ms Lisa Scaffidi, the Lord Mayor of Perth WA and the Council's Chief Executive, paid a fleeting visit to Perth in 2008, and were entertained at Perth's best restaurant – *Deans*. There is also a

Welcome message in lights at No. 1 Middle School, Haikou.
© Andy Chan.

The official banquet with exquisite entertainment from the Martial Arts, and other groups.
© Andy Chan

The entrance to No. ! Middle School, Haikou.
© Andy Chan

strong relationship between the Concert Hall in Perth WA and our concert hall here in Scotland. (See p. 114).

Over the five years of the city status campaign much was done to strengthen these links, bringing significant economic and cultural benefits to Perth and Scotland. As Provost it was my privilege and pleasure to visit all of our official twin cities and welcome their representatives to Perth to take part in the important celebrations. This brought Perth to the attention of our parliamentarians at all levels (Scottish, UK, and European), to British and foreign diplomats, Consuls general and civil servants and others who were involved in developing international cultural and economic links. Ensuring that this cadre of influential people noticed Perth was an important part of the strategy.

Military

Perth's geopolitical situation had ensured its military importance for 1,000 years until the mid-18th century. Now, its military interests are focussed on the Royal Regiment of Scotland, and in particular on the 3SCOTS Battalion, the former Black Watch Regiment, and the TA battalion, 7SCOTS, the 51st Highland Battalion. 7SCOTS was created after the amalgamation of the TA battalions of the Gordon, the Seaforth and the Argyll & Sutherland Highlanders, along with, of course, the Black Watch and it is based in Perth. Furthermore, its title perpetuates

the famous '51st Highland Division' name.

During the Second World War the Black Watch was the leading element of the 51st Highland Division, which is commemorated by the famous War Memorial by the sculptor Alan Herriot on the North Inch. This statue is of a kilted Highland Division soldier, accepting a rose from a Dutch girl. He is carrying bagpipes but not a gun.

Two casts of the memorial were made. The first to be unveiled was at Schijndel in the Netherlands, on the 24 October 1994, the 50th anniversary of the liberation of that small town by the 51st. The Perth statue was unveiled on the 50th anniversary of VE day on the 8th May 1995, by the then Provost of Perth, Jean McCormack.

During the five years leading up to the successful award of City Status,

there were a number of very important military events, which enabled Perth to highlight these historical links, emphasise its ongoing importance to the British Army and raise its profile in military and political circles.

Homecoming Parades After tours in Afghanistan, homecoming parades were held in 2009 and 2012 by 3SCOTS, and also, in 2009, by the Royal Scots Dragoon Guards. Perth is in the centre of the recruiting area of the Black Watch (Perthshire, Dundee, Fife and Angus), and is regarded as its spiritual home. The existence of the Black Watch Museum in Balhousie Castle, which holds the records of every soldier who served in the Black Watch in the

last 250 years, ensures these strong links continue.

The Royal Scots Dragoon Guards recruit from all over Scotland, but usually confine their Homecoming parades to Scotland's central belt. The Lord Lieutenant of Perth & Kinross, Brigadier Melville Jameson, was instrumental in securing their parade in Perth on this occasion. He had served in the regiment and commanded it from 1986–1988, and latterly was the Colonel of the Regiment.

These parades were proud but poignant events. At each event, after marching through the town, past cheering crowds, the soldiers heard speeches from the Provost and the Commanding Officer at a reception in the foyer of the Concert Hall. During my speech at the first Black Watch Homecoming, I read out the names of six young men who had lost

their lives during the tour, and they were remembered. Thankfully, although there were some very serious injuries, there were no fatalities during the tour of the Scots Dragoon Guards, nor of the second Black Watch tour.

The other major military event during this time was the *Award of the Freedom of Perth* to 7SCOTS, (the Highland TA battalion) on 8 May 2010. The Black Watch Regiment was granted the Freedom of Perth in 1947, in honour of its illustrious service during the Second World War.

7SCOTS, on the other hand is a territorial, not a regular, battalion. Territorial soldiers are no longer the part time army that some may imagine. A TA soldier who is called up for duty will spend six months of intensive full time military training, followed by a six-month deployment to the war zone. Whenever a regular

Perth & Kinross Council
The City of Perth

To 51st Highland, 7th Battalion The Royal Regiment
of Scotland

We, the Provost and Members of Perth & Kinross Council, appreciating the glorious traditions created by your most distinguished regiment, The Royal Regiment of Scotland and its predecessors, over many years of loyal and devoted service to our Queen and Country, and in recognition of your long historical association with the City of Perth and its hinterland,

Do by these presents confer upon you the Freedom of Entry into the City of Perth on ceremonial occasions, with bayonets fixed, drums beating, and colours flying, in pursuance of a resolution passed by Perth & Kinross Council on Wednesday, the Thirtieth Day of September, Two Thousand and Nine.

In witness whereof we have caused the Common Seal of the Council of Perth & Kinross to be affixed below, this Eighth Day of May, Two Thousand and Ten.

Provost

Chief Executive

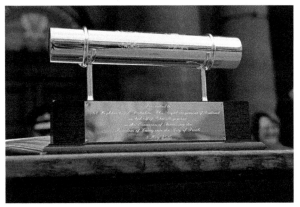

The Freedom of Perth certificate.

The silver casket containing the Freedom of Perth certificate.

Scottish battalion was sent to Iraq or Afghanistan, a detachment of the TA went with them.

When deployed in the war zone they are dispersed alongside their regular comrades, rifleman next to rifleman, and bombardier beside bombardier. They performed exactly the same tasks, and ran exactly the same risks. By the end of the War in Afghanistan over 60 per cent of TA soldiers had served either in Afghanistan or Iraq, and they have had their share of casualties and fatalities. This was the heroic and honourable service that Perth was acknowledging in the Freedom Ceremony.

With TA soldiers now carrying out full battlefield duties side by side with their regular comrades, it was appropriate to award them the Freedom of Perth as well. The occasion was the *Homecoming* of a detachment of TA soldiers from a six-month tour of Afghanistan.

There are two very different concepts of the Freedom of a City. The first is an honour granted by a city to an individual as a mark of special respect or thanks. Sir Stanley Norrie Miller, and Arthur K Bell are among the distinguished citizens of Perth to have been granted this honour.

The second is the modern equivalent of an ancient honour, granted by a City authority to a martial organisation, allowing it to march into that city, 'with drums beating, colours flying, and bayonets fixed'. The custom dates back to Roman times, or even before, when fortified towns would not permit a company of soldiers to enter its gates armed and in formation. This was to protect the town from a military *coup d'état*.

However, a company of soldiers which had given heroic service to a city, and whose honour was beyond question, might be granted the Freedom of that City, and would not have to disarm and break ranks before the gates of that city were opened to them. That is the ancient honour that Perth granted to the Black Watch regiment in 1947, and to 7SCOTS in 2010.

For this occasion the TA detachment assembled on the North Inch, and marched, with colours restricted and bayonets sheathed, to King Edward Street, where they formed up in front of the old City Hall. As Provost, I officiated at the ceremony and presented the certificate to Brigadier Grant, who received it graciously on behalf of the Battalion. Then, on the orders of their Commanding Officer, bayonets were fixed, and the colours released, and the parade, led by its pipe band, set off through Perth to the North Inch. There the soldiers were presented with medals gained for service in Afghanistan, and after a picnic lunch took part in a Highland Games. In the evening the Pipe Band played a Beating Retreat ceremony outside the Concert Hall.

Military Reunions

June 2008 saw the *Final Reunion of the 51st Highland Division Veterans Association* – a sad event full of poignancy. It was held on the same weekend as the Annual Conference

of the Royal British Legion Scotland, which ensured a very large attendance. The weekend began on the Thursday evening, 5 June, with a reception in the Royal George Hotel. On the Friday morning, the Veterans paraded past a saluting dais in front of the Council offices to St John's Kirk, where a Service of Remembrance took place, and wreathes were laid.

The rest of Friday and Saturday were taken up with the Legion's conference, concluding with an official dinner in the evening.

Sunday began with a second parade to St John's Kirk for a service during which the new Tapestry commemorating the 51st Division, was dedicated. The central area of

The programme for the event, and the Order of Service.
© Angus Findlay

Old soldiers reminisce before the Remembrance service in St John's Kirk.
© Angus Findlay

Dedication of the Tapestry. the Tapestry is draped over the Communion Table.
© Angus Findlay

The 51st Highland Division Tapestry now hangs in St John's Kirk, adjacent to the Shrine.

the tapestry depicts an outline map of Scotland showing the main recruiting areas of the 51st Highland Division. Round the periphery are scenes illustrating the life of the soldiers of the 51st Division while on war-time service.

The 51st Highland Division flag passing Alan Heriot's statue of a Dutch girl handing a flower to a kilted soldier.
© Angus Findlay

From the Kirk the Veterans proceeded to the North Inch for the final reunion ceremony in front of Alan Heriot's statue.

Never before had such a galaxy of high ranking military officers been assembled in Perth, and they were complemented by civic and Parliamentary representatives from all over Scotland and from Europe. Delegations from the major recruiting areas of the Highland Division were all present, including the Lord Provost of Dundee, and the Provosts of Angus, Fife and Stirling, along with several Lords Lieutenant. The Provost of Inverness attended accompanied the Mayor of St Valery-en-caux, in Normandy, who laid a wreath. St Valery, which is now twinned with Inverness, was where the 152nd and 153rd Brigades of the 51st surrendered in the dark days of 1940, after a desperate, but successful, rearguard campaign to protect the beaches of Dunkirk.

Four years later, following the D-Day landings, the 51st returned to liberate the village, and its victorious pipes and drums marched down the shattered main street. Several of the soldiers who were captured at St Valery and spent the next five years as POWs and others who took part in the liberation of the village, were present.

Also attending was Mr Eric Berger, the retired Burgermeister of the Dutch village of Gennep, from which the 51st Division initiated *Operation Plunder*, the huge Allied offensive to cross the Rhine and begin the final phase of the War. Mr

Berger presented a bronze plaque inscribed with the names of the 46 men of the 51st Division who died in that short but fierce battle, along with the crests of the units in which they served. I was privileged to receive the plaque on behalf of the people of Perth and it is now mounted on a granite column adjacent to the statue.

Another Final Reunion was held in 2009 – this time of the Scottish Area of the *Burma Star Association*, whose colours are laid up in the Shrine of St John's Kirk. It was attended by Viscount Slim, the son of Field Marshall William Slim, who had commanded the 14th Army during the Burma campaign. This was often called the 'forgotten war', and many Burma soldiers felt that their campaign and sacrifice had never been properly honoured.

The Kohima Memorial in the Burmese jungle.
Courtesy of the Commonwealth War Graves Commission.

Royal British Legion Scotland lapel badge, 2010

Burying the Perth800 time 'capsule' on a dreich November day.
Courtesy *Perthshire Advertiser*.

Plaque marking the site of the buried time capsule.

During this final ceremony for the remaining veterans, all of whom were in their 80s or 90s, the epitaph on the Kohima memorial in the Burmese jungle was read out:

> *When you go home,*
> *tell them of us and say,*
> *'For your tomorrow,*
> *we gave our today'.*

It was all very moving.

Veterans' associations Perth has had a long association with the Royal British Legion Scotland and the Royal Air Force Association of Scotland and Northern Ireland, both of which hold their annual conferences in Perth. These conferences, which are also attended by senior serving and retired officers, involve church services, an official dinner and parades through Perth by the veterans. Each year the Royal British Legion Scotland produced an enamel lapel badge for their delegates. For their 2010 conference they combined their logo with that of Perth800 to produce a very attractive badge, which should become a collector's item in due course.

As well as being the 800th anniversary of the King William the Lion Charter, the Autumn of 2010 was the 70th anniversary of the Battle of Britain, perhaps the most important battle in UK history since Culloden. Mr Gair Brisbane, Director of the Royal Air Force Association, suggested burying a time capsule on the North Inch, with the expectation that it should be recovered in 200 years' time on the 1,000th anniversary of the Charter. The concept was developed into a schools project, and the 'capsule', in fact more like a huge steel coffin was filled with artefacts relevant to Perth and Scotland, mostly provided by primary school children.

Royalty

We were very conscious of the importance of royalty in the City Status competition. While the award of City Status is made by HM The Queen on the advice of her ministers, we were assured by numerous sources that the Queen's opinion would be very important. Our objective was to ensure that Perth was talked about in Royal circles. During the important later stages of the campaign we were able to secure two visits from Prince Charles, Duke of Rothesay (and a third meeting which took place in Holyrood House in Edinburgh), one visit from Prince Edward, and three from the Princess Anne, the Princess Royal.

When the Royals visit, they are generally accompanied by members of their household staff, senior members of the establishment, and sometimes by senior politicians and military officers. None of these people ever left Perth unaware of our ambition.

Advocates for Perth

A unique element of our strategy that was to prove crucial later in the campaign was the appointment of Advocates for Perth. We identified, early in the campaign, that one of Perth's weaknesses was that influential people in London knew very little about Scotland and next to nothing about Perth and its role in Scottish history. *Advocates for Perth* was a targeted campaign to rectify that situation. The Advocates were a cadre of prominent men and women with Perth connections, who were influential in London. They included senior politicians from all parties, peers, eminent journalists, lawyers, academics, businessmen and others, all of whom had informal contacts among those who might be involved in the City Status discussions and decision.

I approached each of them individually, almost all face-to-face, and asked if they would lobby discretely for Perth's City Status claim whenever an opportunity arose. I suggested that this should be on a low key, casual, one-to-one basis. The purpose was to increase the general awareness of Perth, and its city status ambition, and counteract the widespread ignorance of Perth's history.

During the Perth800 campaign, I was fortunate to meet a couple of members of the household staff of Prince Charles, Duke of Rothesay. I took the opportunity to write to them, seeking their discrete support as Advocates for Perth. I was aware, of course, that Civil Service protocol would not allow them to agree. However, my letters were fairly short, and covered the main points of our campaign. If they were read, and I am sure they were, then it was 'mission accomplished'.

Being an advocate was an entirely unofficial arrangement. There were no formal appointments and no reports back. But of course, our advocates were briefed about Perth's history and developments in the City Status campaign, and kept up to date as the campaign developed. Baroness

Veronica Linklater, a Liberal-Democrat peer, whose home is near Perth, agreed to lead this part of our campaign in London and keep us informed about the mood of the movers and shakers who would influence the advice that would eventually be given to the Queen. Pete Wishart, Perth's Westminster MP, was our man in the House of Commons. He cultivated a wide circle of supporters for Perth among MPs of all parties, and led the more overtly political aspects of the campaign

There is, of course, no hard evidence about the effectiveness of our Advocates. However, I believe that in the early stages of the campaign, up to the spring of 2011, their efforts prepared the ground for Perth in a way that could not have been achieved by any other means. Then later on as the tension grew during the winter of 2011–2012, with fierce lobbying on behalf of the main contenders, their contribution to the success of our campaign was absolutely critical (See p. 142)

Homecoming baton passed to Perth800

Before the official Perth800 programme started, I was delighted to be invited to an unexpected ceremony. This was the final event of the Year of Homecoming, held in the Scottish Parliament on the evening of St Andrew's Day 2009. At it, Alex Salmond, the First Minister, handed over a ceremonial baton to me, as Provost of Perth and Kinross, saying

that he was proud to pass on the spirit of the Homecoming to Perth800. He said he was sure Perth800 would bring great economic benefits to a beautiful part of Scotland. It was clear that he was aware of our City Status ambition and was well informed about our plans, including our Westminster Dinner in London. This was to take place the following week, and he wished us well in our endeavour. Within the baton was a copy of the King William the Lion Charter, emblazoned with the Perth & Kinross Coat of Arms, the Perth800 logo and the Homecoming logo.

This was a welcome indication that our efforts to raise awareness of Perth, of its long history, and of our campaign for City Status, were enjoying success, and had been noticed at the very centre of political authority in Scotland.

Edinburgh had been won over – London was next!

CHAPTER FIVE

The first application and the Westminster dinner

London, however, was not going to be so easily conquered.

We anticipated that in 2010 the pace would quicken, and we hoped that the Perth800 programme would build on the Homecoming events and raise Perth's profile ahead of the City Status application. However, before that happened there was an unexpected and unwelcome development, which necessitated a complete revision of the strategy.

Westminster's Opposition to the Civic Honours competition

While the programme for the Year of Homecoming and plans for Perth800 were progressing very well, there was, by the summer of 2009, some anxiety among those of us preparing for the City Status campaign. There had been several briefings about the forthcoming Diamond Jubilee celebrations (still three years away), but none of them had mentioned a civic honours competition. On previous occasions, in 2000 and 2002, there had, by this time, been advance notice of the competition so that potential applicants could plan their campaigns. We were especially worried because the feedback from

Pete Wishart MP and from Baroness Linklater was that in both Houses of Parliament, many members, and especially ministers, felt that there were enough cities already, and that any positive feeling of wellbeing engendered by the competition would be outweighed by the negative political backlash form unsuccessful candidates. And so in July 2009, I wrote to Michael Wills MP, Minister of State at the Ministry of Justice, the Government department in charge of planning the Diamond Jubilee celebrations, to find out what, if anything, was happening. I was dismayed to receive a fairly curt reply stating that there were no plans for a civic honours competition in 2012.

A fundamental reassessment was required.

The First Application

The news that there was to be no civic honours competition dropped like a bombshell into the Council offices at 2 High Street, Perth. The competition had underpinned the Council's whole strategy – the Year of Homecoming; the year-long celebration of Perth800; the application for City Status. Without the competition, much of the steam would go out of the many celebrations planned. Worse, we had started to appreciate just how important city status was, and how disadvantaged Perth would be without it. This was a competition we had to win, and we were going to leave no stone unturned to do so. Now the rug was being pulled from under our feet.

However the research into previous City Status awards had revealed the precedent set by Cambridge in 1951 which gave us a glimmer of hope. As noted briefly in Chapter three, Cambridge had received a charter (now lost) from

King Henry I sometime between 1120 and 1131, about the same time as Perth's first Royal Charter from King David I. However, it was less generous, and some rights granted were later withdrawn. In 1201 King John, under pressure from the burgesses of Cambridge, granted a further Charter, a Certificate of Incorporation, which confirmed the competence of its borough court, and gave rights and liberties to the burgesses. It also established the Merchant Guild, in much the same way as the King William Charter established Perth's Guildry

Palace of Westminster.

Incorporation. In 1951 Cambridge applied for City Status as part of the celebrations of the 750th anniversary of this event. This was granted because of the history, administrative importance and economic success of the town. These historic and economic circumstances were very similar to Perth's current situation.

A possible way forward was to emulate Cambridge and refocus the City Status campaign, not so much on the Diamond Jubilee, but on the Anniversary of King William the Lion's Royal Charter of 1210.

We had been planning to celebrate the beginning of the Year of Perth800 with a major publicity event early in 2010, so it was decided to upgrade the event and stage it in London. We would combine it with the launch of our City Status campaign document, and an announcement that we would submit a petition to the Lord Chancellor requesting that Perth be recognised as a City as part of the celebrations of the 800th anniversary of its Royal Charter.

The headline justification for the request would be that Perth had for six centuries been the capital of Scotland, and thereafter had been designated Scotland's Second City, and was now the modern, dynamic, outward looking administrative centre of a large area of the country. It deserved to be recognised as an official city. Pete Wishart, Perth's Westminster MP, offered to host a dinner in the Palace of Westminster for the event.

A London venue was important for the launch of the City Status campaign because the recommendation to be passed to Her Majesty would be composed by politicians and civil servants who lived and worked in London, many of whom would not be familiar with Perth. The hallowed surroundings of the Palace of Westminster would be the ideal setting for a formal dinner. It would set exactly the right tone and emphasise to guests how important this event was for the future of Perth. The inclusion of the Perth800 programme on the agenda would enable us to demonstrate the strong community involvement in civic matters which is typical of Perth, and the importance of Perth's overseas, military and royal connections.

The First City Status Claim Document

The production of this document was hugely important because it had to embody all that Perth was and wished to become, and pitch it to a sceptical audience. And it had to be produced very quickly, in time to be launched at the Westminster dinner on the 7th of December.

When completed, the Campaign Document consisted of 28 pages with over 60 illustrations in landscape format, slightly larger than A4. It was designed in house, with the design flair that we had come to expect, and printed in Perth. It exuded quality. Copies can be seen in the AK Bell library.

Since this was not a competition there were no stated criteria to fulfil, but we were well aware of the

Tay Street and the Perth Bridge in the evening – the very essence of the City of Perth.

Courtesy of Louis Flood.

requirements that had been specified for the previous competitions in 2000 and 2002. These were fairly broad. In essence the assessors would be looking for a town:

- that was the administrative, legal and commercial centre for a large area;
- that was a regional centre for health and education;
- whose economy was strong and growing;
- that had a distinct identity, and a strong cultural emphasis;
- whose Council was ably led and financially strong;
- that had strong royal, and where appropriate, military connections.

The document dealt in some detail with the particular historical events which we believed justified the unique nature of our claim, and proclaimed that Perth was seeking *restoration* of its ancient city status.

It noted that Perth is the undisputed county capital of one of the largest local authorities in central Scotland, comprising several ancient burghs, each the centre of a large rural area, but looking to Perth for leadership and direction. Furthermore, Perth provides the administrative, legal, commercial, educational and health facilities required for what is a significant proportion of the population of Scotland.

The headquarters of Perth & Kinross Council are at the very centre of the city as they have been since the time of King William the Lion. The Sheriff Court occupies a prominent site on Tay Street, once occupied by Gowrie House, one of the prestigious private houses in mediaeval Perth.

The document noted Perth's royal and military connections, and emphasised its continuing importance as a transport hub. It listed some of the major industries headquartered in Perth, including Stagecoach, Highland Spring, the Morris Leslie Group, and Scotland's largest private company – Scottish and Southern Energy. It is also home to the UK head office of Vector Aerospace. Remarkably, although Perth & Kinross has no coast line, it is nevertheless the base for the Scottish head office of the Royal National Lifeboat Institution, due no doubt, to its hub position in Scotland's transport network.

The HQ of Perth & Kinross Council.

The mirror glass façade of the Royal National Lifeboat Associations Scottish operation.

Perth's Sheriff Court overlooks the River Tay.

The late 15th century tower and spire of St John's Kirk, which would have been familiar to John Knox.

It described and illustrated Perth's main historic and cultural establishments, in particular St John's Kirk, the Fair Maid's House, Scone Palace, the Museum and Art Gallery, the Fergusson Gallery, the AK Bell Library, Perth Theatre and the new

McDiarmid Park, home of St Johnstone FC.

Concert Hall. It elaborated on the main cultural events which take place annually, and gave an insight into Perth's civic society.

The document noted that Perth is the home of many prominent sporting organisations including a Premier League football club and one of the best racecourses in the North of the UK. The head office of the World Curling Federation is located in Atholl Crescent, and Perth is home to the Royal Perth Golfing Society, which in 1883 became the first golf club in the world to gain royal patronage. Perth's modern sports facilities host numerous regular national and international championships from curling to bowling and from golf to volleyball.

In education and academia Perth and Kinross was on the threshold of an exciting new future:

- Six new community campuses had either been built or would be completed by 2011.
- Perth College had received full accreditation as part of the University of the Highlands and Islands.
- The headquarters of the Royal Scottish Geographical Society had moved from Glasgow to Perth. (see p. 128).

In tertiary health care Perth's Royal Infirmary (PRI) had been linked to Ninewells, Dundee University's teaching hospital and medical school, to form one facility on two sites. In mental health, the Murray Royal Hospital had been replaced by a completely new

modern facility, including one of only three medium secure units in Scotland. (See p. 131).

In the City Status competitions of 2000 and 2002, the adjudicators were interested in the leadership and financial strength of the Council. Perth & Kinross Council was well placed in this respect, for the Audit Commission had recently commented very favourably on the political leadership of the Council, noting the good working relationships between the politicians and the executive, and the fact that the opposition leaders and parties were consulted and

involved. Furthermore, an analysis of the Audit Commission's reports into 27 of Scotland's 32 councils showed that Perth emerged as THE leading council by a significant margin. At that time Perth & Kinross was the only Council ever to receive an 'Excellent' mark for financial management from the Audit Commission.

We hoped that our document would circulate within the Ministry of Justice and the Scottish Office, and that it, along with the press coverage of our launch, would alert ministers and others (even members of the Royal household) to our ambition.

The Dinner

The date of the dinner was critical. If it was to launch Perth800, it could be no later than January 2010. However, a General Election was due in May 2010, and we felt that after the Christmas recess, most MPs would be concentrating on their prospects for re-election, and be unreceptive to matters concerning a small Scottish town far away from their constituencies. And so, notwithstanding the difficulty of getting everything ready on time, 7 December was chosen as the date.

It was agreed that we should withhold the formal application until early in the New Year in order to pre-empt a reflex dismissal of our claim and allow time for the relevant parties to see the Document and the Perth800 programme, and take note of the media attention that we hoped our dinner would generate.

On the Friday before the Dinner,

Pete Wishart MP (SNP), Gordon Banks MP (Labour), Michael Fallon (Conservative) and Lord John Thurso MP (Liberal Democrats), tabled the following Early Day Motion in the House of Commons:

Perth800 and City Status:

> This House looks forward to the series of events to celebrate 800 years since the granting of the city charter to the Fair City of Perth; notes the varied and exciting programme of events involving community, cultural and sporting organisations throughout Perthshire; believes that the profile of Perth and Perthshire will be greatly enhanced by the 800th anniversary celebrations and will properly acknowledge Perthshire as a superb tourist destination and desirable place to live; hopes that the celebrations will enhance the campaign to have Perth acknowledged as Scotland's 7th city and looks forward to Perth securing that full city status in its 800th year.

The motion was later signed by a further 25 MPs.

During the afternoon of the 7 December, Gordon Banks, the Labour MP for Ochil and South Perthshire, Pete Wishart MP and I visited the Scottish Office at Dover House, and met Ms Ann McKeachen MP, the Minister of State at the

Scottish Office. We outlined Perth's case to her, and presented her with copies of the Campaign Document and the programme for Perth800. However, it was a disappointing meeting. She said that she would not support an application unless it was part of a competition. Nevertheless, Michael Wills MP, the Minister of State at the Ministry of Justice, had made some encouraging remarks to Pete Wishart and Baroness Linklater, so we were not too downcast.

The guest list for the dinner was very important indeed. We wished to spread the message about Perth as widely as possible, and so would need to select those with a clear link to the decision making process, and a demonstrable connection to Perth.

Those attending were:

From the House of Commons: Gordon Banks MP, Michael Fallon MP and Stewart Hosie MP.

From the House of Lords: Baroness Linklater, Lord Patel of Dunkeld and Lord Peter Fraser.

From Holyrood: Richard Lochhead MSP, representing Alex Salmond, the First Minister, Christopher Harvie MSP and Lord John Thurso MSP.

From 'Civic Scotland': The Rt Hon Lord Gill, the Lord Justice Clerk, Mr John Vine, the chief Inspector of the Border Agency, and former Chief Constable of Tayside, Ms Mandy Exley, Principal of Perth College.

From the Media: Mr Murray Thomson from DC Thomson, publisher of *The Courier*, Mr David Perry from the *Aberdeen Press &*

Some of the guests at the Westminster Dinner.
Back row: Brigadier Jameson, Lord Lieutenant; Lady Provost, Sara Hulbert; Council Leader, Ian Miller; Baroness Linklater.
Front row: Gordon Banks MP; Provost John Hulbert; Pete Wishart MP; Michael Fallon MP.
Image courtesy of the Courier.
© DC Thomson & Co. Ltd

Journal and Gordon McMillan, Head of STV News.

The hosts for the evening from Perth & Kinross Council were spread around the table, and included Pete Wishart MP, myself as Provost and my wife, the Lady Provost, Mrs Sara Hulbert; Mr Ian Miller, Leader of the Council; Brigadier Melville Jameson, the Lord Lieutenant of Perth & Kinross; Ms Dorothy Fenwick, former Head of Publicity, as well as the Chief Executive and the Head of Education and Children's Services.

Those who were invited, but did not attend included Jim Murphy MP, Secretary of State for Scotland; Ann McKeachen, the Minister of State at the Scottish Office; Michael Wills MP, the Minister of State at the Ministry of Justice; Lord Jamie Lindsay, President of the Royal Scottish Geographical Society; Viscount Chelsea, Commanding Officer of 7SCOTS; Sir Michael Peat Private Secretary to Prince Charles, Duke of Rothesay; and Mr Mark Leishman, a member of Prince Charles's staff, who later became Principal Private

Secretary when Sir Michael Peat retired. For reasons of protocol several of these individuals were quite unlikely to be able to accept the invitation, but it kept them informed about the vigour of our campaign for Perth.

All those who were invited received a copy of the Claim Document, and the Programme for Perth800, which listed over 100 events, large and small from all across Perth and Kinross.

In my speech of welcome, I outlined the historical basis for Perth's claim for City Status, and the reasons why we thought City Status was so important. I told them that we had anticipated a competition, which was now not going to happen and so were following the precedent set by Cambridge, and claiming the restoration of City Status as part of our 800th anniversary celebrations.

The dinner went very well. The food and wine were excellent, and the conversation and questions about City Status were lively and demonstrated a genuine interest.

The Aftermath

Over the next few days, the press reports in the UK broadsheets and especially in the Scottish newspapers were very favourable. But more important was the feedback from the 'Westminster Village' through Pete Wishart and Baroness Linklater. This confirmed that we had created a genuine stir in Parliament, and that many MPs and Peers had expressed an interest in our campaign.

However, most surprising of all

was the e-mail I received from Peter Mandelson MP, the First Secretary of State in Gordon Brown's Cabinet. It arrived on 3 January, less than a month after our dinner (a month which included the Christmas and New Year holidays). In it he made no mention of the Government's earlier e-mail which had stated unequivocally that there would be no Civic Honours competition, but reported briefly that the Queen's Diamond Jubilee would be celebrated by:

1 Having an extra public Holiday in June 2012.

2 Striking a medal.

3 Having a competition for Civic Honours. For the first time the Civic Honours competition would include City Status and the Lord Mayoralty (in England, Wales and Northern Ireland), and the Lord Provostship (in Scotland).

There was, however, a sting in the tail of the message. The First Secretary wrote that our application based on acknowledging Perth's 800th anniversary would not be entertained. Furthermore, he also stated that there would be only one successful candidate for City Status, and one for the Lord Mayoralty, from the whole of the UK.

With hindsight it is quite clear that, although the early plans for the Jubilee celebrations did not include a Civic Honours competition, Perth's high profile determination to pursue the matter as part of its 800th anniversary celebrations and cite the Cambridge precedent, induced the

Government to change its mind. This happened because Perth conducted the campaign with as much publicity as possible. We took it to the heart of the Government in London, and enlisted some powerful establishment support. Without the 'noise' and 'chatter' emanating from Perth and echoing around the country, nothing would have happened. Quiet diplomacy and polite letters of protest or complaint would have been ignored. In political terms it was a remarkable 'U' turn, for which Perth can claim the credit.

Nevertheless, the scale of the new challenge was daunting. We had been fairly confident that we could win in Scotland, but to win the sole prize against the might of several huge English towns would be much more difficult.

Notwithstanding Peter Mandelson's e-mail, the Council had already decided at a Council meeting to submit the claim in January, and so we went ahead with the formal request to the Lord Chancellor (Mr Jack Straw MP) on 15 January 2010, along with copies of the Claim Document, which had been launched at the Westminster Dinner.

Predictably the request was refused with an e-mail stating that all applications for City Status would have to go through the competitive process. Nevertheless, lodging the application did ensure that our Claim Document was seen by another different group of civil servants and politicians and that Perth was noticed once again. And so our application was not pointless. It served to develop Perth's reputation, already well established, as a determined candidate for City Status.

CHAPTER SIX

2010 – The year of Perth800: Civic Events

River Tay frozen.
The river is low, as is usual in very cold weather, as the water is locked up in snow and ice upstream.

New Year 2010 came in with the coldest weather for many years, with the Tay frozen except for a narrow channel where the current was strongest. We had recovered from the Westminster Dinner and the refusal of our first Civic Honours application. Preparations for the biggest year of events that Perth had ever experienced were already in full swing. We realised that City Status was very far from the minds of Westminster politicians, who were preoccupied with the forthcoming general election, but in Perth it influenced every decision. We knew now that we would be preparing another application and that the competition was likely to be extraordinarily tough. And so we were determined to use the events of our Perth800 year to promote City Status for Perth, locally, across the UK, and especially in London. We believed that London was the key. Our objective was to impress those who might be able to exert influence on the result and they were predominantly based in London.

The Perth800 Programme

From an early stage it became clear that there would be many very varied events competing for space in the Perth800 programme. Some of these would be important in Scottish and even UK terms, while others would be quite local. To provide a framework which would give the programme shape and impact, the Council sponsored five civic events at strategic intervals throughout the year – in particular a launch in February, a peak event in July and a finale around St Andrew's Day in November, and two other events in June and September to ensure the programme did not sag.

Launch event: Skin and Bone: Life and Death in Mediaeval Perth

The launch event for Perth800 was a major exhibition based on Perth's unrivalled archaeological remains. It was set in Perth's Museum and Art Gallery and was at once spectacular and dignified, and it set the tone for the rest of the year. The guest of honour at the reception, both opening the exhibition and announcing the beginning of Perth800 was Ms Fiona Hyslop MSP, the Minister for Culture in the Scottish Government.

In her speech Ms Hyslop praised the ambitious programme of events planned by Perth & Kinross Council to celebrate the anniversary of the King William the Lion Charter (which was on display), and expressed the hope that our claim for City Status would be successful.

Above
Poster for the Skin and Bone exhibition.

Top left
The Museum and Art Gallery, specially floodlit for the occasion.
© Angus Findlay

Middle
Outside the Museum there were displays of juggling with torches.
© Angus Findlay

Bottom
Opening of the Skin and Bone exhibition. With the Culture Minister, Ms Fiona Hyslop MSP, and Mfrs Sara Hulbert, the Lady Provost.
© Angus Findlay

The main exhibition covered the mediaeval period – from the 11th century, at the time of Malcolm Canmore, when Scotland was consolidating its position as the first nation-state of Europe, until the Union of the Crowns in 1603. During that time, Perth was at the geopolitical centre of the country, at the lowest crossing of the Tay and the farthest point inland of navigation for sea-going ships. It also controlled the gap in the Highland Fault where the Tay pierced the mountains to provide a route to the north and north west. Scone was where the Kings of Scotland were inaugurated, and a few miles to the south was Forteviot, the site of the royal palace. Nearby there were major religious centres at Scone Abbey, and Abernethy. For most of the first half of that period, Perth was the place where the King and court generally resided, and was therefore, *de facto* the capital of Scotland.

Perth is built on a thick layer of silt which has proved to be an excellent preservative for the artefacts and remains of our ancestors. Even fragile fabrics have survived in the waterlogged, anaerobic conditions beneath the foundations. It is also the best excavated mediaeval town in Scotland, and the remains discovered are among the best documented. In particular, the excavation of the Marks and Spencer site on the High Street between 1975 and 1977 (picture page 12 of this chapter) was one of the largest urban mediaeval excavations ever carried out in Scotland, and is unparalleled in terms of the depth, quality and quantity of archaeological deposits revealed. Further detailed excavations were carried out when the St John's Centre was built in the 1980s and before the Concert Hall was built in 2003–2004.

In 2008 the importance of these discoveries was recognised by the Scottish Government, when the museum's entire collection was designated a 'Recognised Collection of National Significance' – the first Local Authority collection to be acknowledged nationally.

The main exhibition was in two parts. In the *LIFE* gallery it celebrated

life of Perth's citizens – their occupations, pleasures, the items that they made, their food and drink, religion and much more. Pride of place in the exhibition was the 1210 Charter from King William the Lion – the basis for our celebration (see Chap 2, 8.11).

The other mediaeval objects displayed represented the core of Perth's archaeological treasures. Prominent among them were two which featured in the BBC's second series of 'A History of the World in 100 Objects'. One was a Pilgrim's badge – a souvenir which a pilgrim to the shrine of St John the Baptist in Amiens in France would have purchased as evidence of the successful completion of his journey. Another was a mediaeval lady's mirror compact. This is engraved with a representation of the romantic legend of Tristan and Isolde in which the beautiful Irish Princess Isolde who is betrothed to the ageing chief Fionn mac Cumhail, elopes on her wedding night with the Fionn's trusted warrior, Tristan.

Upstairs in the Rotunda, beneath the Museum's main dome in the *DEATH* gallery, the objects related to death, disease and crime. The excavations of grave sites have revealed numerous skeletons, some of people

A mediaeval Pilgrim Badge originating from the shrine of St John the Baptist (Perth's patron saint) in Amiens in France.
Courtesy Perth Museum and Art Gallery, Perth & Kinross Council.

Bottom

Pewter mirror case illustrating the legend of Tristan and Isolde.
Courtesy Perth Museum and Art Gallery, Perth & Kinross Council.

Bottom right

Examining a well preserved mediaeval skeleton.
© Angus Findlay

who had met a violent end and others bearing the signs of still recognisable diseases. There were also graves of their pets, particularly dogs.

A third gallery housed an exhibition of Scottish Masters 1750–1850 built around five paintings from the National Galleries of Scotland, which had been touring Scotland during the Homecoming Year, and reflected the five themes of the Homecoming:

Ancestry: The family tree of the House of Glenorchy, by George Jameson.

Robert Burns: A portrait by Alexander Naysmith, (See Chap 4. 1.2).

Whisky: A Brawl Outside an Alehouse by Alexander Carse.

Golf: A Portrait of William Inglis by David Allan, and

The Enlightenment: A Portrait of David Hume by Allan Ramsay.

These five paintings were complimented by a further 32 exhibits from Perth's own rich collection including paintings by Allan Ramsay, Henry Raeburn,

Lady in Blue, By Allan Ramsay. The identity of the lady is not known, but it disbelieved that she was from the Perth area.

View of Perth from Boatland, by Perth artist and photographer, David Octavius Hill (1802-1870). The view shows a very calm river, with the North Inch, the city skyline and the Perth bridge beyond.
Courtesy Perth Museum and Art Gallery, Perth & Kinross Council.

Perth's Museum and Art Gallery with its ionic columns and dome.

David Octavius Hill, David Wilkie, and Alexander Nasmyth.

In an important way Perth's Museum & Art Gallery was itself part of the exhibition. It is a building that is 'Perth' from its foundations to

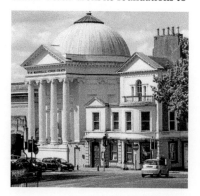

its two domes, and is probably the oldest museum building in the UK still used for its original purpose. The eastern part is based on the Pantheon in Rome, and is referred to as the Marshall Monument, after Thomas Hay Marshall, and entrepreneur and former Lord Provost of Perth. The architect was David Morison, the secretary of the Perth Literary and Antiquarian Society. It was enlarged to the west in 1835, and incorporated a second glazed dome over the entrance hall [6.9]. The extended building was opened by the Duke and Duchess of York, later King George VI and Queen Elizabeth. John Gifford, in the 'Perth and Kinross' edition of the *Buildings of Scotland*,

describes it in glowing terms as 'authoritarian civic architecture'.

June Event: The Official Visit by Prince Charles, Duke of Rothesay on 1 June 2010

Brigadier Melville Jameson, Perth's Lord Lieutenant, was our conduit to the Royal Family, and made strenuous efforts to bring royal visits to Perth during the five years of our Perth800 and City Status campaign. In this he was remarkably successful, securing two visits by Prince Charles, three by the Princess Royal and

several by Prince Edward. Following the success of the campaign HM The Queen came to present the Letters Patent to the new city in 2012.

On 1 June Prince Charles, Duke of Rothesay came to Perth specifically to celebrate the 800th anniversary. The Prince is no stranger to Perth, having been involved in a number of specific Perth projects over the years. Among his engagements on this visit, he was able to review two of them, as well as meet huge numbers of ordinary citizens, and encourage us in our pursuit of City Status.

Perth Railway station

The Prince alighted from the Royal Train at Perth Railway Station, where the Lord Lieutenant and I were privileged to welcome him to Perth. Everyone is aware of his interest in historic buildings, and so

Glazed dome over the new museum entrance.

Below left
The Lord Lieutenant of Perth & Kinross, Brigadier Melville Jameson, CBE.

Below right
Prince Charles is welcomed to Perth by the Lady Provost.
© Angus Findlay

we used the occasion to make a brief presentation of a plan to restore Perth's Railway Station to its former Victorian glory. During the late 19th century, when Perth was at the centre of a veritable spider's web of railway lines, the original station was greatly expanded, and the splendid 1849 building was hidden from view by the construction of an additional north-south line and associated platforms and roofs. Nevertheless, except for its huge porch, the Victorian structure is still intact and could be restored if the 1895 additions, which are now redundant, were removed, and the original north-south line reinstated.

Perth & Kinross Council have drawn up a draft plan for this project, which would provide space for a new bus station, creating an integrated transport hub. However, it would require the co-operation of Network Rail and a lot of money. We had a small exhibition set up on the platform and were able to present it to Prince Charles in order to alert him to the station's potential. Sometime in the future we might be able to enlist his support.

Stanley Mills

Prince Charles's first official engagement was at the 'A' listed Stanley Mills, an enormous water powered mill first built in 1786 on a peninsula jutting into the Tay, some seven miles north of Perth. The oldest part of the mlil, the Bell Mill, is probably the best surviving example of an Arkwright-designed mill in the world. During its 200 years of almost continuous production until it closed in 1989, the complex suffered many fires and floods and challenging

changes in demand and technology. These included a switch from natural fibres to acrylic, and from water wheels to hydro-electric turbines. In 1995 following another fire and considerable decay, it was taken into care by Historic Scotland which began the process of restoration.

In 1997 Prince Charles founded the Prince's Regeneration Trust with the aim of restoring historic places to active and relevant community assets. Later that year Stanley Mills became the Trust's first project. Despite huge challenges, the restoration was successfully completed, converting the Bell Mill into an important visitor attraction, the East and Mid Mills into flats and houses and the installation of new hydro-electric turbines which now export power to the National Grid.

In 2009 the Stanley Mill was successful in the Conservation Sector of the first European Union Competition for Cultural Heritage and achieved the *Europa Nostra Award*, which had been presented to Stanley Mills at a ceremony in Sicily. Prince Charles, who had visited the site in 1997 when it was derelict, was very keen to view the transformation.

The Prince met Mr John Swinney, the local MSP, and was introduced to a number of officials from the Princes Regeneration Trust and Historic Scotland. He then embarked on a tour of the site, which included an inspection of two of the apartments in the Mid Mill accompanied by their owners.

Perthshire Farmers' Market

The Prince's next engagement was a visit to the Perthshire Farmers' Market. His interest in the journey taken by food from the farm gate to the consumer is well known and he has been keen to support moves to reduce the time and complexity of this process. He was aware that Perth was the first place in Scotland to introduce a regular farmers' market (in 1999), and that, since then, it has gone from strength to strength. It is now a farmers' co-operative providing top quality local food that customers trust, and it has spawned a significant number of spin-out farm related businesses, farm shops and restaurants. It is notable that footfall and takings in the city centre shops are better on market days, than on other Saturdays.

The massive six storeys of the Bell Mill at Stanley Mills. It is now a museum.

EUROPA NOSTRA
The Voice of Cultural Heritage in Europe.

The Mid Mill was converted into flats and apartments – some with balconies and others with small gardens, looking out over the Tay.

Jim Fairlie, one of the founders of the Perthshire Farmers' Market, shows the Prince and the Lady Provost some of the lamb sourced from his Perthshire hill farm.
© Angus Findlay

'It was this big. Honest!' Prince Charles talks about fishing at the fishmonger's stall.
© Angus Findlay

The Prince was mobbed by admiring youngsters.
© Angus Findlay

Perth's carilloneur. Dr Ian Cassells, at the clavier (keyboard) in the tower of St John's Kirk.

For this special Farmers' Market a cooking demonstration using local produce was set up, featuring the Michelin Starred chef from Gleneagles, Andrew Fairlie. In all there were 23 stalls, including lamb from the farm of Jim Fairlie, brother of Andrew (above) one of the instigators of the market, smoked salmon, fruit wines from Cairn O'Mohr, bread from local wheat, stone ground at the Blair Atholl Water Mill, Summer Harvest oil from rape seed crushed on the farm, soft fruit, venison, wild boar, and much else. The event was a huge success. Crowds surged around the Prince to his evident pleasure, although some of his security men looked a little concerned.

While the Prince was touring the Farmers' Market, Dr Ian Cassells, carilloneur at St John's Kirk, played a

medley of tunes on the kirk's bells. These included music written for bells by Handel and Purcell, as well as Scottish. Irish, and English traditional melodies.

The Black Watch and Balhousie Castle

The next visit on this busy day was to the Black Watch Castle and Museum at Balhousie. The Black Watch was first raised in Perthshire (in Aberfeldy) in 1739, and has always considered Perth to be its spiritual home. Military reorganisation has meant that the regular Black Watch is now the 3rd Battalion of the Royal Regiment of Scotland (3SCOTS) and the Territorials are part of the Highland Territorial Battalion (7SCOTS). However, the Black Watch spirit, epitomised in its crest, which overlooks the entrance of the castle, lives on and Prince Charles is its Colonel in Chief.

The crest of the Black Watch, on the wall overlooking the entrance to Balhousie Castle. It shows St Andrew with his cross, and the motto, *Nemo me immune lacessit*, surrounded by a laurel wreath. Above is the crown, and below the sphinx, all superimposed on the Star of the Order of the Thistle.

Balhousie Castle was built in 1631, but was greatly modified in the Scots Baronial style in 1863. Thereafter it had a succession of owners, the last of which was the Army. Following a reorganisation of the Army in the 1960s it became the home of the Black Watch Association, and housed the Black Watch Museum and the records of every Black Watch soldier since the regiment was first raised. However, the building was not fit for these purposes, but with ownership firmly held by the Army, and no security of tenure, little could be done. In 2008 the Association launched an ambitious appeal for £3.5m to buy the castle from the Army, extend and redevelop it, and equip it with modern facilities to conserve and display its priceless contents. The Prince was a Patron of this appeal.

And so an important purpose of his visit was to meet the Trustees of the Appeal, and to be briefed on its progress. During the visit he also

Saltire flying proudly above Balhousie castle.

presented the Elizabeth Cross and
Memorial Scroll to two families of
soldiers killed in battle, and the
Afghanistan campaign medal to a
soldier who had been wounded in
Afghanistan. He then met a number
of regular and territorial soldiers and
reviewed a display by the Cadet
Outreach project.

It is worth noting that the
Balhousie Appeal was successful, and

in 2013 Prince Charles returned to
Perth to perform the official opening
of the refurbished castle and
museum. Since then the Museum has
become a very successful five star
visitor attraction, bringing many
thousands of tourists to Perth.

Reception at Scone Palace

The Prince's final engagement was a
reception held in the Long Gallery at
Scone Palace. He left Balhousie
Castle by car, to a send-off by
Kinnoull Primary School pupils, and
arrived at the Palace to a welcome by
flag waving pupils from the Robert
Douglas Memorial School in Scone.
He was greeted at the door of the
Palace by Lord and Lady Mansfield
and members of their family, and
then proceeded to the Octagon room
for refreshments.

Over 200 guests, representing
every sector of civic society in Perth
were assembled in the Long Gallery,
where nine windows overlook Moot
Hill and the replica of the Stone of
Destiny. They were gathered in
groups of ten, each group with a
leader. The Lord Lieutenant and I
conducted the Prince around the
room introducing him to each leader,
who then presented the members of
the group to the Prince. He spoke to
every single person in the room, and
was able to conduct meaningful
conversations with each group – an
impressive *tour de force*. During
these exchanges City Status was
mentioned on many occasions, and it
was clear that the Prince was well
aware of our ambition.

At the conclusion of the reception

referring to our 800th anniversary, and to our claim for City Status.

His last act at Scone Palace, before departing for Edinburgh, was to plant a Cedar tree on the side of Moot Hill.

The Perth Weekend Friday–Sunday, 2–4 July

The first weekend of July was the apex of our celebrations of Perth800, and saw another programme of events, which concentrated on Perth's Royal, military and overseas connections and celebrated everything that was important to Perth, historically, culturally and economically. HRH Prince Edward, Earl of Wessex, was the guest of honour and took the salute at the huge parade.

The date coincided with Armed Forces Day, which is celebrated across the UK, and enabled us to get support for our programme from all three of the Armed Services.

The weekend began on the

I spoke of the strong connections between Perth and Prince Charles and members of his family extending back for generations. I presented the Prince with a glass paperweight, specially designed to celebrate Perth800, and created by Sarah Peterson, the chief Designer of Caithness Glass. A limited edition of 15 paperweights were produced, of which the Prince was given the first. He then gave a gracious speech of thanks,

Clockwise

Prince Charles speaking at the Scone Palace reception
© Angus Findlay

The Prince discusses economic issues with Cllr John Kellas and Ken MacDonald, head of Economic Development.
© Angus Findlay

Caithness glass paperweight.

Prince Charles plants a cedar tree on Moot Hill.
© Angus Findlay

Leading the Civic Parade were the Perth & District Band, and the Spessart Highlanders (in the white shirts).
© Angus Findlay

Right

Michel Gourinchas, Mayor of Perth's twin town of Cognac, carries the French tricolour sash.
© Angus Findlay

Bottom right

The Canadian contingent proudly carry the flag of the Town of Perth in Ontario. This features its coat of arms, and the White trillium, the official flower of Ontario.
© Angus Findlay

Thursday with the arrivals of the Mayors and their delegations from our twin cities of Aschaffenburg, Cognac, Bydgoszcz, Pskov, and Haikou in China, and from our 'daughter town' of Perth in Ontario. Some of these cities, in particular Aschaffenburg and Perth, Ontario, sent large delegations, many of whom had visited Perth before, and were keen to renew acquaintances. The official guests were accommodated in the Royal George Hotel, which was the venue for an informal buffet supper on that first evening.

With the delegation from Aschaffenburg was a pipe band, the Spessart Highlanders, which takes its name from the Spessart Hills, a mountain range close to Aschaffenburg. They have long standing links with the Blairgowrie & District and the Vale of Atholl pipe bands, and took part in the Civic Parade the following day.

Service of Thanksgiving, and the Civic and Military Parades

Friday, 2nd of July was designated 'Perth Day', and the occasion for the main Perth800 celebrations. involving two parades: civic and military. It started in the morning at the Council Headquarters with the civic parade marching to St John's Kirk for an ecumenical Service of Thanksgiving for the 800th anniversary of Perth's Royal Charter.

This parade consisted of the Provost, the Lady Provost, councillors accompanied by their spouses, the Lord Dean of Guild, Lady Mansfield, senior council

officers, and all the overseas delegations. It was escorted by Perth's High Constables, and led by the Perth & District Pipe Band, augmented by the Band of the Spessart Highlanders.

The service was conducted by Right Rev. John Christie, the Moderator of the Church of Scotland, and assisted by the Right Rev. Vincent Logan the Roman Catholic Bishop of Dunkeld, and by the Rev. David Chillingworth, the Episcopalian Bishop of St Andrews, Dunkeld and Dunblane, whose throne is in St Ninian's Cathedral in Perth. Also involved were the Rev. Jim Wallace, minister of St John's Kirk, and Rev. Derek Lawson, the Moderator of Perth Presbytery. It was a memorable service with one of the lessons being read by Herr Werner Elsaesser, the Burgermeister of Aschaffenburg.

Following the service the civic parade marched from the Kirk, by a circuitous route through the streets of Perth to the Promontory at the foot of the High Street, where the dais had been erected. There it disbanded and the various mayors and other dignitaries assembled beside the dais to await the armed forces parade.

Meanwhile, HRH Prince Edward had arrived at Scone airport, where he was met by the Lord Lieutenant of Perth & Kinross, Brigadier Melville Jameson, and was taken to Kincarrathie House in Bridgend to present Duke of Edinburgh Awards to young people from Tayside. He was also introduced to the Chairman and trustees of the Gannochy and

Aschaffenburg Councillors Maria and Johannes Piochotta (centre).
© Angus Findlay

Service of Thanksgiving: Ministers taking part (from left to right): Rev. Derek Lawson, Bishop Chillingworth, Rev. Jim Wallace, Bishop Logan, and Rt. Rev. John Christie.
© Angus Findlay

Prince Edward and Brigadier Jameson, the Lord Lieutenant.
© Angus Findlay

The combined Pipes and Drums of 7SCOTS and 3SCOTS set out from the North Inch.
© Alasdair Wylie

The first Guard of 3SCOTS turn the corner from the High Street into King Edward Street.
© Angus Findlay

other Trusts, the Lord Dean of Guild, and officials involved in the Duke of Edinburgh Awards Scheme. He then proceeded to the Promontory overlooking the Tay, where he met the senior Army, Navy and Air Force officers involved in the parade.

At about this time the armed forces parade was setting out from the North Inch to march via King Edward Street and South Street to Tay Street and the Promontory, where Prince Edward was to take the salute. It was led by the combined pipes and drums of 7SCOTS and 3SCOTS – in all about 50 musicians.

The armed services followed in order of seniority – first the Royal Navy including a large contingent from No. 45 Commando based at Arbroath. The Third Battalion, the Royal Regiment of Scotland (3SCOTS), formerly the Black Watch, was next and contributed by far the largest contingent. Their commanding officer, Lt. Col. Fenton was parade commander, and he led the 1st Guard of 75 soldiers, which was followed

by the Colour Party, and then the 2nd Guard also of 75 soldiers. The Black Watch Regiment was granted the Freedom of Perth in 1946, and so these soldiers marched with fixed bayonets which glinted in the bright sunlight.

After the Army came a sizeable contingent from the Royal Air Force, and then the Regimental Military (Brass) Band of the Royal Regiment of Scotland, and the Highland Band. In all about 350 serving soldiers, sailors and airmen took part.

After the servicemen there were two large groups of Veterans, including the Royal British Legion (Scotland) Pipes and Drums; followed by Cadets from the Navy, Army and Air Force; Scouts and Guides; and finally a group of veteran World War II vehicles. The total of 1,000 marchers made this the largest military Parade in Scotland in 2010.

As the leading bands approached the saluting dais, a G4 Tornado from RAF Leuchars carried out a low flypast, its noise drowning out the pipes and drums. This was followed by a Spitfire piloted by Iain Hutchison from the Scottish Aero Club at Scone. This drew much applause from the crowds.

The Parade marched to the North Inch and was followed on foot by Prince Edward, who then presented the Elizabeth Cross, to members of the families of six soldiers killed on

active service. Thereafter representatives from the groups taking part in the parade were presented to the Prince.

Museum Reception

While the soldiers and others from the Parade were served a packed lunch on the North Inch, the Prince was taken to the Museum, where he toured the Skin and Bone Exhibition, and after a private lunch he signed the Guildry Locket Book (see Chapter 2).

After lunch I gave a speech of welcome to our Royal guest, and presented him with the second of our Perth800 paperweights. I remarked that the room in which we were standing was part of the extension to the Museum and Art Gallery, that had been opened by his grand parents, the Duke and Duchess of York, later King George VI and

Queen Elisabeth, almost exactly 75 years previously on 10 August 1935.

I was also able to give some hard economic facts to the audience, which included many senior business and professional people from Perth. Figures presented to the Council earlier that week had shown that in

for the whole Perth800 programme, and this weekend in particular, was to reinforce the foundation for a formal bid for City Status in the Civic Honours competition, which we expected would be held to celebrate Her Majesty's diamond jubilee.

It was the right time to welcome, officially and introduce the Prince to the delegations from our twin cities and other officials and guests. The overseas delegates were excited, as only foreigners can be, at the opportunity to shake hands with a member of the Royal Family. I also presented another Perth800 paperweight to the Rt. Rev. John Christie, who had conducted our Thanksgiving Service.

Prince Edward then proceeded to circulate around the room, speaking to everyone, before making a gracious speech, thanking the people of Perth for the great welcome, and for the magnificent parade.

Perthshire on a Plate

He then departed to visit the Concert Hall and open the *Perthshire on a Plate* exhibition. This was a two day celebration of the quality products of Perthshire, particularly food and drink. Among others he met Sarah Peterson of Caithness Glass, who created the Perth800 paperweights. Thereafter he departed with the Lord Lieutenant to tour the Game Fair which was being held at Scone Palace.

Beating Retreat

Later in the afternoon the Military (Brass) Band of 3SCOTS, and the

the year 2009/10, which had included the latter part of of the Homecoming year and the first few months of Perth800, events and conferences had attracted additional net revenue of £16m to Perth & Kinross, which was three times more than the previous year.

I emphasised to His Royal Highness that an important objective

Pipes and Drums of 3SCOTS and 7SCOTS performed a combined Beating Retreat outside the Concert Hall. During this display two young soldiers performed a very athletic Highland Dance. It was an unequalled display of Scottish military music and dancing.

For the final event of the day John Chan, the leader of Perth's Chinese community, entertained the civic party and the official delegations from our twin cities with a Chinese meal in the Jade Garden Restaurant in Scott Street.

Saturday 3rd and Sunday 4th of July

The following Saturday and Sunday were much less hectic. On the Saturday the visiting delegations and

councillors involved in the various twinnings had a tour of the Aberfeldy Distillery and then lunch in the Kenmore Hotel. The weather was kind, and on the way they saw some of the beautiful scenery of Highland Perthshire. In the evening there was a Ceilidh in the Dewars Centre.

On Sunday there was an optional visit to the Game Fair at Scone Palace, and then a formal lunch for the overseas delegations at the Murrayshall Hotel, at which official gifts were exchanged. In the evening the March Mellows, a street band

The Military Band of 3SCOTS Beat Retreat outside the Concert Hall. The Pipes and Drums await their turn in the background.
© Angus Findlay

from Aschaffenburg entertained the crowd, and then there was a concert in the Concert Hall, staged entirely by local talent, and compered by the Perth born singer Donald Maxwell. Perth & Kinross Youth Orchestra played a major role, but there were contributions by choirs and bands from across the Council area. In the evening farewell drinks were served in the Royal George Hotel, and the following day the various delegations departed.

It was a remarkable weekend, and was well covered by the local press. It provided many, many opportunities to network on behalf of City Status. The Diamond Jubilee was still almost two years away, but we knew that other candidate towns in England were beginning to prepare, and we were determined to lead the way.

September Event
Perth: A Place in History

In the Autumn of 2010, Perth & Kinross Heritage Trust, an 'arms length' organisation of the Council, held a two-day conference, *Perth: A Place in History*, which examined Perth's development and its outstanding contribution to Scotland's history.

Papers were presented by 12 distinguished scholars – academics,

Perth: A Place in History. The Conference in full swing.
© David Strachan, PKHT

Enthusiastic conference goers browse the exhibits in the Concert Hall foyer.
© David Strachan, PKHT

The Carpow Log Boat is the second oldest log boat found in Scotland and is one of the best preserved in the whole of the UK.
© David Strachan, PKHT

A picture of the excavation of the Marks and Spencer site, revealing the extend and depth of the work.
Courtesy Derek Hall, Scottish Urban Archaeological Trust.

historians, archivists and archaeologists – from Perth, the rest of Scotland and the USA. The proceedings were published within the year, and included a comprehensive summing up by Professor TC Smout, HM Historiographer Royal for Scotland. The contributions demonstrated, according to Professor Smout, 'a vibrancy of research scholarship', which spanned the millennia from mesolithic times to 2000 AD. He noted that the area is rich in ancient settlements – Scone, Moncreiffe, Forteviot, and Abernethy, but that Perth itself was relatively late on the scene. Perth had developed when communication within Scotland and with the outside world began to be important for the development of the area, causing the River Tay to become both an obstacle to cross and an arterial route for trade, for civic and religious diplomacy and military deployment.

The range of contributions was very wide. David Strachan, archaeologist and manager of the Perth & Kinross Heritage Trust set the scene, with a paper entitled, *Before the Burgh: 15,000 Years of Crossing the Tay*, which explained the topography of the Tay estuary as it emerged from the last ice age. He led us through the Neolithic and Bronze ages to the Picts and Scots who inhabited the area after the Romans withdrew. One of their notable legacies was a bronze age log boat which surfaced on a mud bank downriver from Perth after some 3,000 years.

Archaeology consultant, Derek Hall, then discussed the extensive investigations that have made Perth the best excavated mediaeval burgh in Scotland. In his paper, *800 Years Under Your Feet – the Archaeology of Mediaeval Perth*, he showed, among many interesting discoveries, that a church had existed where St John's Kirk now stands, much earlier than the 12th century which had previously been the accepted date.

In *Perth in the Middle Ages – An Environmental History*, Professor Richard Oram of Stirling University, examined a topical new angle on the underlying factors affecting Perth's development. He discussed the effect of climate, famine

and disease – not just on the people of Perth but on the surrounding rural population of people and animals, on which Perth's economy depended.

The paper by Dr Alan MacDonald. *Perth and Parliament, c1300–1707*, has already been cited in Chapter 2, as evidence for the *de facto* status of Perth as Scotland's capital in the first half of the 15th century.

Town Life and the Life of the Town in the Sixteenth Century, the contribution by Mary Verschuur, (Perth born, but from the University of Nebraska), took the audience on a walking tour of Perth as it would have been 400 years ago. She enlivened the commentary with many anecdotes of common life which have percolated through the dry tomes of history.

Professor Christopher Whatley in his paper *Perth in the Era of the Enlightenment* wrote, 'There is no good reason why 18th century Perth

shouldn't be as well known by historians as other leading Scottish towns'. Referring to Perth's Georgian developments overlooking the North and South inches he states, that, 'Perth could boast not one but two new towns', and also that it, 'had become one of the more genteel of Scotland's provincial towns'. The contribution from the late Professor Charles McKean from Dundee is titled, *The Anglification of Perth?* (note the query), and it is a little at odds with some of Professor Whatley's conclusions. He notes how Perth was very much a working town with smoke stacks rising behind the genteel Georgian terraces.

Perth's geopolitical situation ensured that it featured on many maps. In *Perth on the Map: A Cartographic Voyage through Time*, Chris Fleet from the National Library of Scotland selected eight maps to illustrate Perth's development through time. He began with Timothy Pont's sketch dated c1599, and worked through different stages of Perth's development up to the first Ordnance Survey map of 1860.

The last section of the conference featured four contributions which dealt with Perth in the 19th and 20th centuries, and in particular with five individuals and families who were instrumental in developing Perth's infrastructure and commerce at that time.

Dr Adam Anderson (1780–1846) was a polymath who was appointed Rector of Perth Academy, but at the same time was an advisor to the

Burgh Council, supervised the introduction of gas lighting to the streets, and constructed a new water supply for Perth. This last enterprise included the building of the waterworks (now the Fergusson Gallery) designed by Anderson in the style of a Greco-Roman temple (see Chapter 14, p. 182). Later, he became Professor of Natural and Experimental Philosophy at St Andrews University.

Sir Robert Pullar was an innovative entrepreneur who, with the help of the railways, expanded his family's cleaning and dyeing company until, in 1909, it employed nearly 3000 people and had over

The Proceedings of the conference: *Perth a Place in History*, edited by David Strachan.

4,700 agencies across the UK. Whisky and Insurance were staple industries of Perth throughout most of the 20th century, and left important legacies from which Perth still benefits. There were contributions dealing with Arthur Bell & Sons, Dewars of Perth, and the General Accident.

The final paper by Roland Bean, the Council's Head of Planning, called *The Future of our Heritage* reassured those attending that Perth & Kinross Council was very conscious of the importance of securing its heritage for the future.

The proceedings have been published in a substantial book, *Perth: a Place in History*, edited by David Strachan. It now constitutes a very valuable resource, and is available from the Perth & Kinross Heritage Trust or the AK Bell Library.

This conference and the *Perth Skin and Bone* exhibition gave the whole Perth800 programme that intellectual rigour and gravitas which was so important in underpinning our claim for City Status.

Finale: The Grand Climax: 21–28 November

The finale of the Perth800 celebrations consisted of a week-long series of events building up to a huge fireworks display over the River Tay on the Friday night, the Light Night Festival at the weekend, and the St Andrews Day service in Dunkeld cathedral. It began in suitably festive frosty weather, but it ended dramatically with a massive snow-fall which completely severed all of Perth's road and rail connections.

Christmas Lights

The week began on Sunday 21 November when thousands of Perth folk turned out to celebrate the official Switch On of the Christmas Lights. The streets were alive with the deafening sound of the Perth

Christmas lights switch on in front of the City Hall. Courtesy of the Perthshire Advertiser

Jambouree Choir at the Christmas Lights switch on. Courtesy of the Perthshire Advertiser

College Samba band, street entertainers, stalls, buskers, and characters from Perth Theatre's Pantomime production, Aladdin.

Radio presenter Ally Bally hosted the show and kept the fast and furious entertainment going with the help of the local band *Vortex*, and the *Jambouree Choir*, led by Edna Auld, until the Switch On itself in front of the City Hall. I was honoured, along with the Lady Provost to flick the switch and light up the streets.

Famous Grouse Statue

The next morning was as cold, dark and dreich as any Scottish November day could be – with a bitter wind, rain and snow. It was the day that Edrington Distillers planned to present the huge *Famous Grouse* statue to the people of Perth, as their contribution to Perth's anniversary.

Perth has an illustrious tradition of public art. John Gifford in the Perth & Kinross volume of *The Buildings of Scotland* states, 'carefully positioned sculpture of the late 20th and early 21st centuries forms a public display of enlightened patronage unrivalled by any other town or city in Scotland' (p 570). I believed that it was very important that Perth's 800th anniversary should have a significant legacy of public art to augment its already impressive collection, and was delighted that two important additions to Perth's canon of sculpture were created to celebrate the 800th anniversary.

A group of five new pillar sculptures were carved along Tay Street flood wall (described in Chapter 10), and Perth's newest, and largest sculpture, an enormous statue of a red grouse taking flight as if from a Perthshire heather moor, was erected in the centre of Broxden roundabout.

The statue commemorates the Famous Grouse whisky blend, first produced in Perth by Matthew Gloag in 1905. The picture of the red grouse on the label was drawn by Philippa, Matthew's daughter, and is still one of the best known trade marks in the industry.

Edrington Distillers is an independent Glasgow based company owned by the Robertson Charitable Trust. In 1999 it took over Highland Distillers (formerly Matthew Gloag & Sons), Perth's last foothold in the whisky industry. For nearly 20 years, Edrington has maintained a presence in the old Highland Distillers head office at Kinfauns, but sadly, following the

Famous Grouse Statue at Broxden.
Courtesy of Edrington Distillers.

construction of a new headquarters building in Glasgow, it will close in 2017.

The statue was constructed by the artist, Ruaraig Maciver of Peebles, by bending and welding heavy steel rods into a huge but very life like shape of a red grouse rising from the moor. It

Scale model of the Famous Grouse statue.

was then galvanised to protect it from the weather, and give it a light grey 'spangle' (to quote the artist). Because of the scale of the work, the tops of the trees on the roundabout appear like the heather beneath the feet of the bird as it takes off.

In view of the wild weather, and because the statue was in the centre of a very busy roundabout, the launch event was a subdued affair. However, a much more conventional occasion had been planned for the following Friday afternoon, when at a reception in the Concert Hall, Mr Gerry O'Donnell, the Corporate Affairs Director of Edrington Distillers, formally presented the statue to the people of Perth. He also presented one of three scale models of the statue to Perth & Kinross Council.

In accepting the gift on behalf of Perth, I noted that the Red Grouse was an iconic Scottish bird, found in Highland Scotland, a few places in England and nowhere else in the world; that along with the heather moors it was ingrained into the cultural psyche of our people; and that as a game bird it was very important to the economy of Highland Perthshire. I noted that Perth had once been at the very epicentre of the Scottish whisky industry, but that time had passed.

Regarding its position at Broxden, I said that the roundabout was close to the pass over the ridge of the Ochil Hills, and that, 'from Roman times onwards, invading armies approaching Perth from the South, came over that ridge and would have paused near to this point, as the city came into view, to survey the landscape and plan their campaign. Now, of course, it is the welcome armies of tourists who swing round Broxden, either to enter Perth, or carry on up the A9 to Highland Perthshire and beyond. They are the lifeblood of our modern economy. And as they pass Broxden, they will see a sculpture that embodies so much of what is important to us in Scotland, in Perthshire, and in Perth itself'.

A week of Events

Throughout the week there was a programme of events and activities, many of which were calculated to stimulate the interest of children in the history of Scotland, and Perth's place in that story.

Scottish Country Dancing

On the Wednesday, over 900 children from primary schools in Perth &

Kinross took part in the St Andrews Day of Dance organised by the Royal Scottish Country Dance Society (RSCDS) and held in Bells Sports Centre. The children had come to show off their dancing skills and to perform new dances just published in the Society's booklet, *Scottish Country Dances for Perth 800*.

When I spoke at the Society's annual meeting in 2009, I suggested that the RSCDS might develop a dance to celebrate Perth's 800th anniversary. This invitation was accepted enthusiastically and a competition was set up, with four new dances being chosen and published in the special booklet.

The first dance in the booklet is a 32 bar reel, *Perth 800*. It was was choreographed by Linda Gaul of Pitlochry to music written by Angela Young of Aberdeen.

Booklet of Scottish Country Dances published by the RSCDS, and containing four new dances, including 'Perth 800', and 'The Buttercup'.

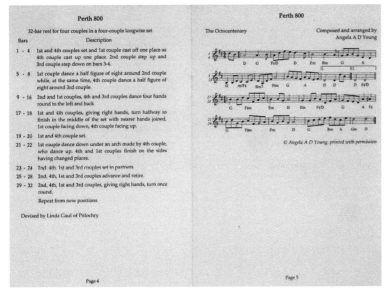

The description and melody for the Reel, *Perth Octocentenary* or *Perth800*, by Linda Gaul.
Courtesy RSCDS

The description and melody for the jig, The Buttercup. Courtesy RSCDS

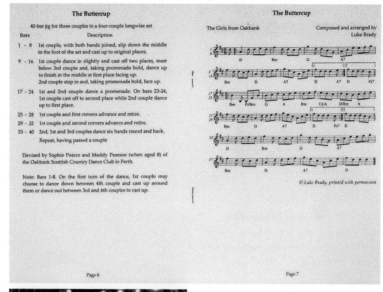

RSCDS Ball 2010. Sophie Pearce & Maddie Pearson perform the Buttercup Dance. Published with the consent of the families of Sophie and Maddie.

Winning design from the Schools Heraldry Competition. Courtesy St John's Academy and Perth & Kinross Council.

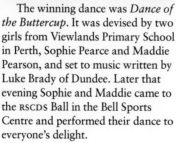

The winning dance was *Dance of the Buttercup*. It was devised by two girls from Viewlands Primary School in Perth, Sophie Pearce and Maddie Pearson, and set to music written by Luke Brady of Dundee. Later that evening Sophie and Maddie came to the RSCDS Ball in the Bell Sports Centre and performed their dance to everyone's delight.

Two other dances are published in the RCDS booklet – *The Swan and the Tay* (a Strathspey) and a reel, *Perth Meets Perth*. Both had been submitted to the RSCDS by members of the Perth, Western Australia, branch of the Society, demonstrating the enormous geographical range of Scottish country dancing.

Scottish country dancing also featured on the Saturday evening on the High Street outside Perth Theatre, along with a special performance of Michael Jackson's Thriller Dance, organised by professional choreographers.

Heraldry competition

Later in the week there were prizes to present for the Schools Heraldry competition – another element in the strategy to teach our children about

Winners of the Art & Design exhibition .
Courtesy *Perthshire Advertiser.*

their history. Pupils had been asked to design a coat of arms, adhering to heraldic rules, which demonstrated what was important to them about their community. The Archive section of the AK Bell library was involved and took very seriously the objective of increasing civic awareness and pride among our young people. The designs showed how worthwhile that had been. The winning design came from Bethany McGrogan of St John's Academy.

The Art & Design Exhibition

Held in the Concert Hall this was the culmination of many months of research, reading, painting, photography model-making, creating banners, and a whole lot more, by several hundred primary school children. The objective was to illustrate who we are, and where we have come from. It was a diverse and fascinating exhibition.

Battle of the Clans

Two days later, over 1,000 Primary 4

Battle of the Clans

The battle ordered by King Robert III in 1396 was to settle an old feud between the clans Kay and Chattan.

Sir Walter Scott used the Battle as the central narrative in his novel, *The Fair Maid of Perth.* In Sir Walter Scott's version 30 men from each clan were pitched against each other in mortal combat on the North Inch, in front of the King and citizens of Perth. Clan Chattan emerged victorious with the last man of the Kay clan fleeing the battle by swimming the Tay. Scott inserted a romantic theme which gave the title to the book. It involved a fair maid, Catharine, the daughter of a well known Perth merchant, Simon Glover, and a local armourer and swordsman, Hal O

the Wynd (Henry of Mill Wynd). Scott, writing 450 years after the event, used as settings for the scenes In his novel the buildings, streets and vennels of Perth as he knew them – and many of them are still recognisable today.

In the novel, Scott referred to Perth as 'The Fair City' over 300 times, and the name has stuck ever since.

boys re-enacted the *Battle of the Clans* in a song and dance spectacle in the Concert Hall.

St Andrews Day Big Sing

Later in the week choirs from all over Perthshire, along with international musicians and celebrity soloists took part in a night of global song performed in English, Gaelic and Mandarin. It lasted from 6.oopm until midnight, with people encouraged to pop in and out during the evening.

The Moon Sculpture

The week was not given over entirely to singing, dancing, noise and children's activities. Horsecross sponsored an exhibition in the Concert Hall by the unconventional Beijing based artist-sculptor Wang Yuyang. For this exhibition, Horsecross brought over from China (at considerable cost) his huge artificial moon sculpture, which was hung in the centre of the foyer. This art work, which measures 13 feet in diameter, and consists of over 2,000 fluorescent light bulbs, was first

Art Gallery Exhibitions

At the same time in the Museum and Art Gallery the *Skin and Bone Exhibition* continued until the end of the year, and there were two further exhibitions, one national, and the other local. The *Trailblazers' Exhibition* highlighted the work of female artists from the 19th century to the present day. Among them was Elizabeth 'Bessie' MacNicol who took the struggle to get women artists acknowledged to Paris at the end of the 19th century. Included in the exhibition was her painting, *Young lady in a sun bonnet*,

exhibited in Shanghai during the Mid-Autumn Moon Festival. It celebrated the moon worshipping tradition in Shanghai during which people burn incense as the moon rises, offer moon-cakes and other delicacies to family members and decorate images of the Moon Palace. Wang Yuyan's moon hung in the foyer of the concert hall for over a year, and is now in storage.

The Chinese artist-sculptor, Wang Yuyang.

The Moon Sculpture, hanging in Shanghai.
Courtesy, Horsecross

Young Lady in a Sun Bonnet, by Elizabeth (Bessie) MacNicol.
Courtesy Perth Museum and Art Gallery, Perth & Kinross Council

(thought to be a self portrait). Another was Dame Elizabeth Blackadder, the first woman to be elected to both the Royal Scottish Academy and the Royal Academy, and since 2001, *Her Majesty's Painter and Limner in Scotland*

Meanwhile in Gallery One of the Museum and Art Gallery the local Perthshire Arts Association held their traditional annual exhibition. A small but important part of this exhibition featured work by art students in Perthshire schools, with prizes for the most exceptional exhibits.

Cittaslow

Over this final weekend of Perth800, Perth's Cittaslow committee hosted both the AGM of the UK Cittaslow Towns committee and the annual meeting of the Cittaslow International Co-ordinating Committee – the first time this committee had met in the UK. Among the delegates present were Gian Luca Marconi, the President of Cittaslow International, and the Mayor of Castelnuovo ne Montio, in Italy. As Provost I welcomed the delegates at a reception in the Council Headquarters on the Friday evening, and also launched their Conference on the following morning. Among the delegates were a group from the Hungarian town of Hódmezővásárhely – quite a mouthful for the Provost to announce! The conference theme was, 'Twenty First Century Towns – Surviving or Thriving?'. It was a wonderful opportunity to promote Perth's ambition to be a dynamic small European city to an international audience.

Artists in Residence

A number of artists spent periods *in residence* in Perth at this time. Among them were two from New Zealand, Ina Edwards and Victoria Johan, who produced videos of their artistic journey from New Zealand to Scotland, and of their experiences in Perth.

Another was artist Jessica Ramm, who was awarded a month-long residency by Perth and Kinross Council, and commissioned: *To build a machine to investigate the eight hundred years of history and to bring them together in a spectacular display of mechanical wizardry*. The result was the weird and wonderful Miraculating Machine, a stamping machine constructed out of bicycle parts and an old tuba, and mounted on wheels so that it could be trundled, noisily, through town.

Light Night/Nuit Blanche/White Night

To bring down the final curtain on Perth800, Scottish and Southern Electricity, Stagecoach and Perth & Kinross Council co-operated to stage a Light Night Festival over the last weekend. The concept of a night time cultural event, with street activities of all types (but especially involving illuminations), and open doors at all museums and galleries until midnight, was first established in Nantes, as *Nuit Blanche* in 1983. Its purpose was to give citizens an opportunity to come together in the evening, rejoice in their city, and focus on their shared history, culture and identity. The concept has spread irregularly through Europe, and notably to St Petersburg, where the annual White Night Festival in June is now an international tourist attraction.

Nevertheless, those who have experienced the warm dark evenings of a central European summer, or even the midnight *simmer-dim* of June in St Petersburg may have had misgivings. To translate that experience to a Scottish city on the 57th parallel in November, required courage, enterprise, a leap of faith, but most of all luck. But how remarkably successful it was!

The City's main public buildings and many commercial buildings were floodlit and in the afternoon, after it became dark, the Tay turned chameleon as its surface shimmered with different colours. A light and audio show flickered on the walls of St John's Kirk and the City Hall, telling the story of Perth over the last 800 years. Outside the Concert Hall there was an interactive kinetic light installation – a space-age engineering wonder where light and pictures were projected from a crane 50 feet above the pavement in response to the movements of people below picked

up by infra-red cameras. The concept had been pioneered in Dublin in 2008, and refined for Perth800.

Fireworks

For more than a week the people of Perth had speculated about the activities of workmen who appeared

St John's Kirk, floodlit like never before.
© Angus Findlay

King Edward Street, Climbing wall Outside the City.
© Angus Findlay

Interactive Kinetic Light installation outside the Concert Hall.
© Angus Findlay

the trees, and because the island flooded at high tide, the fireworks were going to be fired from pontoons floating on one of the fastest flowing sections of the river. Fireworks being set off from the middle of a wild river like the Tay! At night! In November!

By 7.00pm on the Friday night, Tay Street had been closed to traffic, and a cover erected over a wide stage mounted on the Promontory. This was to protect the members of the Perth Symphony Orchestra, the Perth Youth Orchestra and the Perth and District Pipe Band, and all their instruments, from whatever the weather might throw at them. A huge crowd had assembled stretching along Tay Street and up the High Street. It was bitterly cold, but dry, and there was no wind. There was a buzz of excitement in the air, and expectations were high.

Across the river, the trees on the east bank were floodlit in many colours, with Kinnoull church floodlit in white light prominent among them. Perth has never seen such a firework display. A waterfall of white light cascaded down from the Perth Bridge onto the water, and from there floated in rivulets of colour down past Tay Street to the Promontory.

The fireworks started with a single explosion, but then erupted from the pontoons on the river, and all of it choreographed to music played by the Pipe Band and the two orchestras, and conducted by Alan Young.

As the fireworks and music reached a crescendo the first snow flakes began to fall. Ten minutes later,

to be building pontoons in the river, between Stanners Island and the Promontory. There was disbelief when they were told that because of

by which time the programme had ended, it was snowing heavily. While musicians warmed up their frozen fingers, the crowd was jubilant, cheering and clapping.

The Andermas Mediaeval Fair

This ancient market traditionally held on St Andrews Day heralded the beginning of Advent and the start of the Christian year. It was widely celebrated in Europe, especially in Russia, Greece, Romania, and of course Scotland, all of which have St Andrew as their patron saint.

In Perth, by the Saturday morning it had stopped snowing, and there

was only a moderate covering, which had been cleared from the streets. There were market stalls of all types, and those selling hot food did brisk business. Members of the Antonine Guard staged re-enactments, and put on displays of arms and armour, while Perth's executioner put in an appearance along with his axe and instruments of torture, and a dragon put in an appearance. Musicians in costume played mediaeval instruments, and there were demonstrations of fish smoking and chestnut roasting. Meantime the cafés and restaurants provided sustenance to keep the revellers going.

The St Andrews Day Service

Each year Perth & Kinross Council holds a St Andrews Day Service on the Sunday nearest that day. It is held in a different church each year, and over the years all denominations have been included. In 2010 it was due to be held in Dunkeld cathedral – a very fitting place to round off our anniversary year.

Snow

On the Saturday evening the weather began to close in again, with more snow. On Sunday, in the morning, the A9 was passable with care, but there were severe weather warnings, and most people from Perth, including the pipe band, and the Provost's official car did not attempt the journey. Nevertheless, I went in a 4 x 4 car, and the service did take place although it was somewhat truncated, and lacked the usual pomp and circumstance.

During that Sunday afternoon and evening Tayside experienced its heaviest snowfall for many years, and all road and rail connections to Perth were cut off, forcing over 700 motorists and other travellers to seek out emergency accommodation in a school provided by Perth & Kinross Council. Hundreds of others were less fortunate and spent the night in their cars and lorries, including the driver of Perth's official car, who kept warm by wrapping himself in the Provost's robes!

It was a very memorable end to a very memorable civic year.

CHAPTER SEVEN

Building the momentum for City Status

While the Council's programme of civic events for Perth800 was very important, we knew that if Perth's profile was to be raised among those who might influence the Civic Honours decision, all sections of the community would have to be seen to be enthusiastic, united and involved. An overwhelming commitment to the Homecoming Year and to Perth800 would help to prove that to be the case.

That commitment was indeed forthcoming, not only for 2010, the Perth800 year, but, beginning with the Homecoming Year (2009), it continued during Perth800 and throughout the City Status campaign until 2012. It was manifest in the number of events promoted during this time. Many, of course, were annual events, some with a long pedigree (such as the curling championships) and some of the 'events', for example the Perth Festival of the Arts, were in effect, programmes within the programme. Without exception, however, the organisers of these annual events made a special effort for Perth800. For the peak year of 2010 over 100 events were accepted onto the official programme.

National and International sporting events

Perth hosts several regular national and international competitions, including the Yonex Scottish Badminton Championships, the Scottish National Bowling championships and the Perth Masters Curling Championships. Others, including the Intercontinental Rally Championship and the Junior Ryder Cup which generally moved around different venues, made a point of coming to Perth in 2010 to contribute to our 800th anniversary celebrations. Two, the Colin McRae Forest Stages Motor Rally and the Johnnie Walker Golf championship at Gleneagles, have recently been discontinued but between 2008 and 2012 they afforded important opportunities for networking on behalf of Perth's claim.

All of Perth's local sporting organisations were enthusiastic. As well as holding local events, several were able to persuade their parent bodies to bring their Scottish, UK and International championships to Perth. The Tug-of-War, Volleyball, Gymnastics and Netball championships fell into this category.

Two major annual sporting events were first established at this time. These were the *Étape Caledonia*, an 81-mile, closed road, cycle race through Highland Perthshire around Pitlochry and the *Tay Descent*, a canoe race from Dunkeld to Perth. These events both have two complimentary strands – a serious race for committed athletes and a challenge for hobby competitors. This has ensured their popularity which has developed steadily, so that they now attract entrants from all over the UK and beyond.

An example of a very local and initially low key project was the *Perth Chess Festival*. This was started by some chess enthusiasts in 2004 as an event to encourage the playing of chess, particularly in schools. However, with help and sponsorship and Perth800 badging, it was built up to a major festival in 2010 and beyond, bringing several international grand masters from as far away as Italy, Denmark and Ireland.

Curling: From the hush of the Chess competition to the *Roarin' Game* – Curling is at the other end of the sporting spectrum. Perth and Perthshire have a long and illustrious association with curling, providing several gold medal winners in recent Olympic and World Championships. It is also the permanent home of the World Curling Federation, the governing body of the sport, which has its secretariat based in an office in Atholl Crescent.

Curling offers huge opportunities to project Perth internationally, especially to northern Europe and Canada. Each January the Perth Masters' Championship brings 16 overseas teams of curlers (and their supporters) to compete with 16 Scottish teams, during the darkest days of the winter, when the shops and hotels are at their quietest.

In 2009, the Perth Masters was followed by the Centenary competition for the Strathcona Cup. This trophy, for a grand bonspiel between Scotland and Canada was presented by Lord Strathcona and was first contested in 1909. The competition takes place every five years, alternately in the two countries. In recent years 60 curlers from each nation have taken part in a round robin of matches across the country lasting six weeks. Over the century the spoils have been evenly divided, with the advantage usually going to the visiting side, which has been playing together as a team over a long period. Canada won in 2009, the Homecoming year, but Scotland

regained the trophy in 2013 in Canada.

Then in 2010 the 20th Curling Fellowship of Rotarians World Championships were held in Perth. This was followed in 2011 by the World Junior Curling Championships which brought young representatives, along with their families and coaches from 12 overseas nations to Perth.

Club and Society events

As well as sporting organisations other local clubs and societies also wanted to be part of the programme. The Model Railway Club, for example, held a special two day exhibition to mark its 50th anniversary bringing visitors from all over Scotland and England. Meanwhile in 2012 the *Philatelic Society of Perth*, which regularly hosts the annual meeting and dinner of the Scottish Philatelic Society, was able to persuade the Association of British Philatelic Societies to come to Perth for their AGM.

On one of these philatelic occasions I was introduced to the after dinner speaker, Lord Gill, the Lord Justice Clerk and one of Scotland's most distinguished legal academics. He was one of many influential people from Scotland and further afield, whom I was privileged to meet during this time. At such encounters I always raised Perth's City Status ambition and expounded the merits of our case and the difficulties we expected to encounter. In the later stages of the campaign, when the odds against Perth seemed

to be daunting, I was able to approach these individuals again and seek their cooperation as 'Advocates' for our cause (see p. 59).

(see p. 59)

Publications: The Perthshire Society of Natural Science (PSNS), established in 1867 and one of Perth's most important intellectual organisations, made two valuable contributions to the Perth800 programme. The first was the 28th volume of the Journal of the Society. It is a significant production devoted to a study of the early maps of Perth from 1715–1902 and consisting of nearly 100 A4 pages beautifully printed on photographic paper and lavishly illustrated with reproductions of the maps. Like the Society's earlier volumes, it is a valuable resource for those interested in Perth's history and development.

The second was an exhibition mounted by the Perthshire Photographic Society, which is a subsection of PSNS. The exhibition,

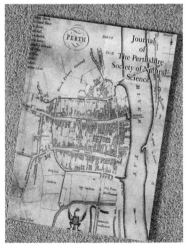

Perth & Kinross Today was displayed in the Foyer of the Concert Hall and consisted of nearly 100 photographs, depicting Perth and Perthshire in every way imaginable. Later in the year the exhibition was taken to Birnam and in 2012 it was mounted in Aschaffenburg – Perth's Bavarian twin city. It was accompanied by a booklet illustrating all the images.

Through the Perthshire Photographic Society, PSNS is continuing Perth's long involvement with photography, beginning with

The 28th volume of *The Journal of the Perthshire Society of Natural Science*. The cover shows a detail of James Stobie's map of Perth in 1783.
Image courtesy of The Perthshire Society of Natural Science

A dramatic picture from Perth & Kinross Today. Taken at sunrise, it shows the Kinnoull Tower overlooking the River Tay in the Carse of Gowrie.
Courtesy Mike Bell, Perthshire Photographic Society

Magnus Jackson and continuing with David Octavius Hill.

Anniversaries

A remarkable number of important anniversaries were celebrated in Perth between 2007 and 2012 and were conjoined with Perth's 800th anniversary and City Status campaign.

Perth Concert Hall: The fifth anniversary of the opening of the Concert Hall fell in September 2010. Conceived in the late 1980s as a Millennium project, the years of planning were dogged with setbacks, including the withdrawal of funding by the Scottish Arts Council. However, eventually the determination of the Perth community, notably the Council and the Gannochy Trust, won through and the Concert Hall was opened by HM the Queen in September 2005.

Contrary to some negative expectations, the ambitious targets set for its first three years were all achieved or surpassed. By 2010 the Concert Hall was a massive contributor to Perth's cultural scene, its architecture and city-scape, its economic success and of course, to its City Status ambition.

And so throughout 2010 there was a series of events which promoted both the Concert Hall's anniversary and Perth800. The most important of these was a concert by the prestigious *Australian String Quartet*. Their programme included the première of *After Silence*, a composition by the outstanding Australian cellist and composer Iain Grandage, written to celebrate the relationship between Perth in Scotland and Perth in Western Australia (WA). The four musicians and their chief executive flew from Australia to Scotland especially for this concert and they presented to Perth a specially bound copy of the music score. The total cost of this event was a gift from the Trustees of the Concert Hall in Perth WA. The trustees had developed a special relationship with their counterparts at the concert hall in their 'mother-town' since they received, due to a postal error, a bill for many thousands of pounds from one of the contractors building our concert hall!

On behalf of Perth, I gave the Quartet one of our specially commissioned Caithness Glass paperweights.

The international nature of this event was enhanced by the presence of members of *L'Association Franco-Ecosaise*, who were spending

Perth Youth Orchestra performed for Her Majesty the Queen and the Duke of Edinburgh at a special opening event at the Concert Hall. Here Alan Young the Director of Music introduces Her Majesty to some of the performers.
Image courtesy of Andrew Mitchell

a week in Perth as the guests of their Scottish counterpart – *The Franco-Scottish Society*.

Heart of Scotland Air Show: The first Air Show in Scotland was held in Lanark in 1910, a mere seven years after the Wright Brothers' maiden flight. Incredibly it attracted over 200,000 visitors to see only seven aircraft. There is now no airfield at Lanark, so Perth Airport at Scone seized the initiative to celebrate this important anniversary and to promote Scone's facilities to the aviation industry and the economic potential of flying from Scone to the Perth business community.

In 2009 the sponsors (Morris Leslie Group, Squadron Prints from Arbroath and the Scottish Aero Club) held the first annual Heart of Scotland Air Show. It was very successful. The Red Arrows performed spectacularly and there were many other flying and static displays.

For the special event in 2010, the Council invited the Lord Provost of Glasgow, whose predecessor in 1910 had supported the original Lanark air show. We also invited the Provost of

South Lanarkshire, the successor to the Provost of Lanark. This was part of our effort to promote Perth's city credentials to other civic leaders and seek their support. Sadly the Red Arrows cancelled due to the death one of their pilots during a training flight, but a Typhoon from the RAF performed spectacularly. There were other flying displays by a wide variety of aircraft, including Russian Yak 52 aerobatic trainers and the Breitling Wing Walkers. In addition

Heart of Scotland Air Show, Scone. Red Arrows above Perthshire.

Heart of Scotland Air Show. Formation flying by the Breitling Wing Walkers.

Microlights are increasingly common in the skies above Scone airfield.

A two seater Hurricane in the hangar at Scone.

Photo finish in the Camel race for the Prince's Scottish charities.
Image courtesy of the *Courier*.
© DC Thomson & Co. Ltd

With the Lady Provost discussing Perth's City Status ambition with Prince Charles. The occasion was the reception in Holyrood house ahead of the Charities race day.
Image courtesy of the *Courier*.
© DC Thomson & Co. Ltd

there was a static display of over 60 aircraft.

Perth Race Course: The Board at Perth Race Course certainly appreciated the commercial possibilities of anniversaries. In 2008 they celebrated the centenary of the change from Flat racing on the North Inch at Perth, to racing under National Hunt rules at Scone Palace Park. Then in 2010 they persuaded the British Horse-racing Authority to grant (in a rare departure from normal practice) an exceptional

licence to hold an extra race day to celebrate Perth's 800th anniversary. At this event, while there was a full race card, there was also a pageant, with King William the Lion arriving in a carriage and presenting a charter to me as Provost of Perth.

Even more remarkable was the Charities Race Day in August 2011 to raise money for Prince Charles's Scottish charities. This was preceded on 1 June by a reception for potential donors in Holyrood House. Both events were attended by Prince Charles, Camilla, Duchess of Cornwall and by Alex Salmond, who on the race day gave up his First Ministerial duties to become a racing tipster! The event, which included a camel race, raised over £200,000 for the Princes' charities.

The Holyrood reception was held just two days after the closing day for applications for Civic Honours, which enabled me to remind the Prince of Perth's interest. And then, on race day, the Lord Lieutenant reminded him again when I was introduced as the leader of Perth's campaign for City Status. The Royal Household was well aware of Perth's ambition.

Perth Racecourse managed to celebrate yet another anniversary in 2013 – the quatercentenary of the

first recorded race in Perth, on the South Inch in 1613.

St Johnstone FC: Not an anniversary but the beginning of a new chapter. St Johnstone, Perth's football club, delighted the whole of Perth and Perthshire by winning promotion to the Premier Division in May 2009 and were paraded through the crowded streets in an open top bus. It was entirely fitting that as a candidate for City Status Perth should be represented on the football field by a Premier Division Club.

Perth Festival of the Arts: This jewel in Perth's cultural crown celebrated its 39th anniversary in 2010 with an outstanding programme. An important highlight was the special Perth800 Concert, with the Royal Scottish National Orchestra, conducted by Sir Andrew Davis and featuring the American soprano, Barbara Bonney. The Festival organisers generously donated a block of 60 seats at this concert to the City Status campaign so I was able to invite our Advocates to a reception and a very special evening's entertainment. They left with a great impression of the cultural offering available in Perth and a pack of information about Perth and City stratus in their pockets.

In the Festival programmes the young musicians of Perth & Kinross are always included. They feature in lunchtime concerts each day and the Perth Youth Orchestra leads the music at the inaugural Festival service.

In 2011, the Festival celebrated its

40th anniversary with another ambitious programme. The highlight was a concert with Joshua Bell and Steven Isserlis and the Orchestra of the Academy of St Martin in the Fields, conducted by Ian Bell. And there was much more – the Bolshoi Symphony Orchestra; Sir Frederick Ashton's *Romeo and Juliet*; Dylan Thomas's *Under Milk Wood*, three operas by the English Touring Opera Company, as well as folk music, talks and art exhibitions.

The Film Festival: The Perth Film Society celebrated its tenth anniversary with a three day Film

Members of the St Johnstone team, with the First Division cup on the balcony of the Council HQ in the High Street.
Courtesy of the *Perthshire Advertiser*

Opening of the tenth anniversary of the Perth Film festival in 2010.
Courtesy of the *Perthshire Advertiser*

The critically acclaimed film, *The Last King of Scotland*, starring James McAvoy, and directed by KevinMacDonald was shown and then discussed at the Perth film festival.

Combined choirs in St John's Kirk: Craigclowan senior choir in front, Stiftsbasilika Kinderchor in the middle, and Perth Choral behind.
Courtesy Ástmar Ólafsson, Craigclowan

Festival over the weekend from the 23 April 2010. It featured films from Rome, Berlin, Paris and of course Perth and celebrated the work of Perthshire educated Kevin MacDonald, who directed the film *The Last King of Scotland*. MacDonald's work was also the subject of an on-stage discussion between Peter Stevenson, the Chairman of the Perth Film Society and Stuart Cosgrove, the Editor of Channel 4 and one of our Advocates. Also shown were a number of short films by Perthshire pupils.

International Musical Events

In addition to the Festival of the Arts programme, there were three very special international musical events. The first, the visit of the *Australian String Quartet*, is reported above.

Ars Antiqua Choir and the Stiftsbasilika Kinderchor: Our twin city of Aschaffenburg has a soaring reputation for music, especially choral music. The ancient Roman Catholic Basilica (which miraculously survived the devastating bombing during the last months of the Second World War) supports both adult and children's choirs.

In 2007 and again in May 2010 the Stiftsbasilika children's choir visited Perth with their charismatic Master of Music Herr Unterguggenberger, as guests of Craigclowan school. They made a huge impression in several venues, including in Perth's St Ninian's Cathedral and the St Andrews Cathedral in Dundee.

Ars Antiqua, is an independent adult choir, which sings *a cappella* music at the highest standard. Germany's international reputation for choral music is sustained by a quadrennial competition in two stages. First, there are the State competitions, then a year later the State winners compete in the all Germany final. *Ars Antiqua* has won the Bavarian competition several times and been highly placed in the All Germany final. These very creditable performances are undoubtedly due to the driving ambition of their professional conductor Stephan Claas.

These visits were not only to Perth from overseas. The Perth Youth Orchestra, the Perth and District Pipe Band and Perthshire Brass and others, have all toured the continent and in the process visited Aschaffenburg and Bydgoszcz on several occasions. Occasionally there was a happy coincidence when a tour coincided with an official visit by a Council delegation.

Scottish Tides – Polish Spring, was the third of the special musical events. It was designed to celebrate the many connections (not all musical) between Scotland and Poland and in particular between Perth and Bydgoszcz, Perth's Polish twin city (see p. 47). These included a concert by the *Filharmonia Pomorska* Bydgoszcz's professional symphony orchestra which had flown over specially for the occasion; lectures by Billy Kay on the Scottish diaspora in Poland, which dates back to the 17th century; and a concert by the Warsaw Village Band. This band actively seeks out and arranges contemporary settings for Polish folk songs and lyrics which are in danger of being swamped by modern Poland's prevailing western culture.

Classical and Traditional Music

Perth has a very strong tradition of classical music with regular performances by the RSNO, the Scottish

Chamber Orchestra and by its own amateur orchestras – the Perth Symphony Orchestra and the City of Perth Sinfonia. That tradition is nurtured by a strong emphasis on orchestral music in the schools, with the Perth Youth Orchestra performing twice yearly in the concert hall.

Ars Antiqua choir with Stephan Claas on the Perth Promontory.
© DC Thomson & Co, Ltd.

Perthshire Brass conducted by George Annan in a concert at the Aschaffenburg Schloss in 2010.

Alan Young conducts the Perth Youth Orchestra in the Concert Hall.
Courtesy of Andrew Mitchell

The 'Trads'. The MG Alba traditional music awards were held in Perth Concert Hall in 2010.

Picture courtesy Louis de Carlo

Traditional music is also strong, with the Scottish Fiddle Orchestra perfuming regularly. In 2010 and again in 2011, the MG Alba Traditional Music Awards, known universally as *The Trads* were held in the Concert Hall, to acknowledge the Perth800 celebrations. While *The Trads* might not be noticed by the metropolitan élite in Westminster, traditional music is very popular and hugely important to Scottish culture. It was rightly prominent in the Perth800 programme.

Johnnie Walker and Blue Grass

Two regular international events held in 2010 were badged with Perth800. which helped with the promotion of the events and of City Status. The Johnnie Walker Golf Championship at Gleneagles, was one of three European tour events which regularly took place in Scotland. It brought to Gleneagles Hotel and to Perthshire the top professional golfers and

thousands of spectators, many of whom found their way to Perth.

At the other end of the accommodation spectrum was the Guildtown Blue Grass festival, which celebrated its 25th anniversary in 2010. This remarkable festival of Blue Grass music, dominated by American and European bands, was held in Guildtown, some ten miles north of Perth. Here, many of the festival goers pitched their tents or parked their caravans in the field behind the Guildtown village hall. The surroundings were certainly not as plush as at the Johnnie Walker championship but the atmosphere was every bit as real and the fun element even greater than at Gleneagles.

Sadly in recent years both these events have been discontinued, having succumbed to the economic downturn.

International *Mega* Events

In 2010 two major international events were held in Perth which brought several thousand competitors and supporters to the city from all over the world – they were the UK Geocaching Mega Event and the Park World Tour.

Geocaching is a modern 'sport' which originated in the USA and has spread widely right across the world. Geocaching participants use hand held GPS devices to get the co-ordinates of hidden containers (caches), which hold items placed in them by other geocachers. They then share their experiences online. The

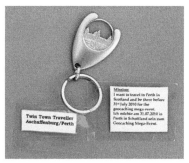

item may be a message, a 'bug', or clues to another cache etc. When members find the cache, they log their find (and any interesting details, photographs or events) on the Internet and then either leave the cache as they found it, or if they remove something from it, they leave something else behind.

One of the main attractions of geocaching is the opportunities it provides to see the sights of the countryside – its castles and churches, waterfalls and bridges, the views of hills, rivers and mountains. Perthshire is rich in all of these. By 2010 there were over one million active caches in the world, on all the world's continents, including Antarctica.

For this event the organisers hid several hundred caches around Perthshire. In one of them was a 'Travel Bug' (a Perth800 key ring) with a message that it was to find its way to the Lord Mayor (Oberburgermeister) of Aschaffenburg.

The first finder of the bug came from Nottingham and took the keyring and hid it in another cache near his home, logging the location on line. In a remarkably short time, it found its way across to Aschaffenburg – each step being logged on the internet for interested people to follow. The finder who was the last link in the chain then met Herr Herzog, the Oberburgermeister, who gave him an Aschaffenburg key ring, with instructions that it had to find its way to Perth by 31 July 2010 for the Geocaching mega event.

It then started on its way back to Perth. This it did remarkably quickly and I met the last finders (a German couple) in my office.

The UK Geocaching Mega Event was a get together of 1,400 geocachers from 40 countries across the world. It was the biggest international 'sporting' event ever held in Perth.

Orienteering is another modern sport which has rapidly grown in popularity. It combines the physical challenge of cross country running with the intellectual problem of navigation and is managed in classes to cope with age groups ranging from 8 to 80! In 2009, the Scottish Six Days Orienteering Festival was held in Kinloch Rannoch and Glenshee in Perthshire and Barry Buddon in Angus. It attracted over 3,000 competitors (and their supporters) from all over the world. However, not many people in Perth would have noticed it, although the proprietors of the camp sites and guest houses in Highland Perthshire certainly did.

The Park World Tour. This is orienteering in a park, such as Scone Palace Grounds, or actually within a city centre, rather than in open country. Athletes use a street map to navigate their own way around the city, carrying an electronic tag which must be verified at each checkpoint. There is no set route to follow – each competitor working out his or her own circuit. The name, *Park World Tour* is derived from, 'a wild idea – a World Cup in Park Orienteering'. The sport was born in Scandinavia in 1996 and has grown exponentially since.

In 2010 international athletes from 17 countries, along with domestic runners who had qualified in a preliminary round at Scone Palace the previous day, competed for the €5,000 prize money in Perth's first Park World Tour event. They raced across town, past shoppers and spectators, up vennels, down lanes and through pedestrian precincts and across streets – all without any mishaps. First places in both the men's and women's races went to Scandinavians, with the Englishman Graham Gristwood coming second in the men's event.

Helena Jansson, the women's winner, commented, 'I have never seen a course like this. It was really tricky with little streets and alleys. It was just the way it should be. I agree that it was more difficult than the world championships. This is a whole different level. You don't get street orienteering like this in Norway'. Quite a compliment!

Twinning Events

Throughout 2010 (and indeed before and since) there were regular visits in both directions between Perth and our twin cities.

One of the most memorable, however, was the *Twinning Olympics*, held in August and involving young people from Aschaffenburg in Germany, Bydgoszcz in Poland and of course, Perth. This was the third *Twinning Olympiad* and on this occasion involved six sports: badminton, football, swimming, golf, table tennis, gymnastics and a Highland Games! On the previous two occasions only Perth and Aschaffenburg were involved but this time Bydgoszcz joined in. While Perth had triumphed in the previous two *Olympiads*, on this occasion Aschaffenburg collected the most medals. After the Games there was a great Ceilidh in the Dewars Centre, which was thoroughly enjoyed by the young people themselves and also by their parents, coaches and other supporters.

Perth and Poland

Poland's strong connections with Scotland led me to attend three special events which cemented the importance of Perth in the relationship between Scotland and Poland.

The first was the *Scottish Tides – Polish Spring* series of events in the Concert Hall including the performance by *Filharmonia Pomorska*, which are noted above.

The second was the *exhumation of Guidon Langer* who had been buried in the Polish military cemetery in Perth and his re-interment with full military honours in Poland.

Langer was a senior officer in the Polish army who, after a notable career in the First World War, was appointed to lead the Polish Cipher Bureau. The Bureau was evacuated to Southern France before the collapse of Poland in 1939 and there he continued to work on the Enigma Code, making an important breakthrough which enabled the cracking of the Code in Bletchley Park When the German military took over Vichy France in 1943, Langer was captured. Although tortured he did not reveal that the Code had been broken. After the war he came to Scotland and died in Kinross in 1948 and was buried in Perth.

The normalisation of politics in Poland after the collapse of the Soviet Union brought about a reappraisal of their military history. Langer was recognised as a hero of Poland and in due course his remains were exhumed and later re-interred in Poland with full military honours.

The third event was an invitation to attend the *70th Anniversary Exhibition of the Polish School of Medicine* in Edinburgh University, which took place on Poland's

The exhumation of Guidon Langer on a bitterly cold snowy day in December 2010. On the left is Dr Tomasz Trafas, the Polish Consul General, and holding the flag is Mr Markek Straczynski, the President of the Polish Ex-servicemen's Association in Scotland.
Image courtesy of The Courier © DC Thomson & Co Ltd.

The shield of the Polish School of Medicine which was situated in Edinburgh from 1941 to 1949. It features the crowned Eagle of Poland, the thistle for Scotland, Edinburgh castle and the serpent and staff of Asclepius the Greek God of Medicine, all emblazoned on a Saltire.
Courtesy Maria Dlugolecka-Graham

The Knight's Cross of the Order of Merit of the Republic of Poland.

Constitution Day, 3 May 2011. The exhibition celebrated the Polish School of Medicine which had operated within the Faculty of Medicine at Edinburgh from 1941 to 1949. Here medicine was taught to Polish nationals (mostly ex-servicemen) in their own language but subject to the academic discipline of Edinburgh University.

Dr Stanislaw Gebertt, (See p. 47) who was instrumental in establishing the twinning link with Bydgoszcz had been a graduate of Edinburgh's Polish School of Medicine.

So far as the City Status campaign was concerned, attending this event was particularly fortuitous because it led to an introduction to Professor Sir David Edward, one of the most eminent Scottish lawyers and a Judge of the European Court of Justice. He later became one of Perth's 'Advocates' (of which more later) and contributed a trenchant comment to the final document submitted in support of Perth's claim.

An honour from the President of Poland. The many and varied links between Perth and Poland in which I was involved, led to an unexpected honour. After I had demitted office, I was informed that the President of Poland had graciously awarded me the *Knights Cross of the Order of Merit of the Republic of Poland*, on the recommendation of Dr Tomasz Trafas the Consul General. The award is made to foreign citizens who have contributed to the deepening of relations with Poland. It was presented by Dr Trafas at a

ceremony in the City Chambers of Edinburgh.

The Environment

East Perthshire is justly famous for its soft fruit. However, the apple, pear and plum orchards along the banks of the Tay have a much longer, if now less well known, history, which extends back to the monasteries of the 11th and 12th centuries. The decaying remnants of one of the largest of these orchards still exists within the city boundary, between the Dundee Road and the Tay, on both ides of the railway line.

Sadly all that remains of the orchards associated with the four religious houses within Perth itself, are street names and even these are

Pears are the most long lived of the orchard trees. This ancient pear tree blooms defiantly in a derelict orchard on the outskirts of Perth.

neglected. Pomarium Street for example signifies the location of the Carthusian monastery's ancient orchard. However although the street exists and is marked on the map, there is no street sign. Nevertheless, the Pomarium Flats, which are entered from the street are signed.

Perth800 Orchard: As part of the widespread resurgence of interest in orchards across Scotland, a group of Perth enthusiasts proposed the planting of a dispersed Community

Orchard of 800 fruit trees to celebrate Perth's 800th anniversary. Batches of apple, plum and pear trees (up to 50 specimens in some locations), were planted in unused pockets of land around schools, in housing schemes and parks and in the grounds of Perth college UHI. Over the next 30 years they will make a big contribution to Perth's urban environment and perhaps also to the diet of some of our children. Contrary to some expectations these trees have survived the vulnerable early years very well, with very few being vandalised.

Support from Trusts and Businesses

The Gannochy Trust was an important sponsor of events of all kinds throughout the Perth800 and City Status campaign. Other local trusts all contributed generously, as did the Guildry Incorporation and the Perth Common Good Fund. Local, Scottish and UK businesses sponsored many events, especially in the Perth Festival of the Arts programme, sporting occasions and the finale of the Perth800 celebrations.

A number of businesses produced specialities to mark the Perth800 year.

Kilt Pins. Two special kilt pins were produced for the anniversary year. The most important of these was the *Cairncross Kilt Pin*. The Jewellers shop, Cairncross of Perth on St John's Street, founded in 1869 and now owned by Mrs Flora Rennie, is

Street sign for the high rise housing development on the site of the orchard belonging to the Carthusian monastery.

A group of 'Perth800' fruit trees flourishing among meadow grasses in a strip of wild land between the Town Lade the park adjacent to the Tulloch housing scheme.

A more manicured Perth800 orchard in the courtyard of Perth College UHI.

The Cairncross Kilt Pin.

The hall marks on the back of the Cairncross kilt pin (see text).

The ancient stamp (hall mark) of the Perth assay office.

Perth800 Kilt Pin by Lorraine Law.
Courtesy of the *Perthshire Advertiser*

The launch of Perth800 Ale in the Cherrybank Inn with the brewery's Fergus Clark, and the owner of the Cherrybank Inn, Jack Findley.
Image courtesy of The *Courier* © DC Thomson & Co. Ltd.

justly famous for Tay pearls. However, for Perth800 Cairncross produced s special silver kilt pin. The head of the pin is surmounted by a heavily textured double headed eagle and on the shaft is the figure '800' in the style of a celtic knot.

The most interesting features, however, are the hall marks on the back of the pin. There are, of course, the normal hall marks for silver designed by Cairncross. These are: the maker's mark ('A & G C' for Alexander and George Cairncross) followed by the silver standard (925), the rampant lion of Scotland, the mark of the Edinburgh assay office (three towers) and the date letter ('I' for 2010). What makes this item special, however, is the use of the old stamp for the Perth assay office.

Perth's earliest hall marks, at the end of the 17th century hark back to Perth's alternative name, St Johnstoun and featured the lamb of St John carrying a banner. However, from 1750 until the office at Perth was discontinued in 1836, silver assayed in Perth carried the double headed eagle mark. Cairncross had to obtain special permission from the Assay Office to use this stamp once again, in addition to the usual marks. And so these silver kilt pins are the first and so far the only items to carry this historic hall mark for nearly two centuries.

While one of the Cairncross pins was donated to the Perth Museum, the production was a commercial proposition and a limited number were produce for sale. In due course they should become collectors' items

Cairncross was not the only company to produce a Perth800 kilt pin. *Lorraine Law*, a local silversmith, produced a one-off piece to celebrate Perth800. The head of the pin features the Perth800 logo, decorated with semi-precious stones. Two of them were made, one of which was donated to the Perth Museum and the other auctioned for funds for the Perth & Kinross Association of Voluntary Services (PKAVS).

Perth800 Ale. Perth's Inveralmond Brewery also acknowledged the importance of Perth's 800th anniversary with a special brew of Perth800 Ale.

Ancient Buildings Restored

Perth was fortunate that a number of major projects which came to fruition at this time involved the restoration of ancient buildings and investing them with exciting new potential. Among these were St John's Kirk of Perth, Balhousie Castle and the refurbishment of the pedestrian precinct in the High Street. Although unrelated to the City Status campaign, these developments, which involved millions of pounds and

many hundreds of people from organisations in Perth and across Scotland, contributed to the feelings of optimism and expectation which infused so much of that campaign and the Perth800 celebrations.

St John's Kirk of Perth. This is by far the oldest building in Perth. There is archeological evidence of a church on this site since the 11th century and documents relating to it in court papers dated 1126–1128. As Perth grew, especially in the mid 15th century the Kirk was extensively reconstructed. The choir, the oldest surviving part of the building was completed in the late 15th century and the tower and spire by 1511. Although the Kirk has been altered or modified in every century since, its exterior would be instantly recognised by the mediaeval citizens of Perth.

The interior of St John's, prepared for a concert with the new chairs, the grand piano on the stage, and spot lighting bar.

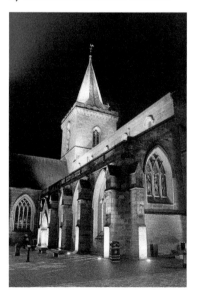

Most recently £2.75m was raised (over £2m from local sources) to make the Kirk fit for its various roles as a modern place of worship, as the focus for many of the most important civic events that take place in Perth, as a venue for concerts and other events and as an important tourist attraction. The heating, lighting, toilets, office accommodation and electronics were modernised and the chairs replaced. The opening service took place on Easter Sunday 2011.

Other ancient buildings which have been extensively restored are described in detail elsewhere. These include *Balhousie Castle* (see p. 81), the *Fair Maid's House* and *Lord John Murray House* (see below).

The Façade Scheme is at the opposite end of the financial scale from the

The choir, tower and spire of St John's Kirk – the oldest parts of the oldest building in Perth.

Several of these businesses in the High Street have benefitted from the Façade Scheme, which provides small grants to properties in conservation areas to facilitate the upgrading of the frontage to the street.

The Brahan Building, the main centre of Perth College UHI.

multi-million pound restorations of listed buildings. Under this on-going scheme small grants are provided by the Perth & Kinross Heritage Trust to assist the upgrading of the façades of shops and other properties within Perth's conservation areas.

Academic

The University of the Highlands and Islands was finally awarded full University Status by the Privy Council, in February 2011 and Perth at last had a university – one of the important, though not essential, criteria for City Status. While the headquarters and the general administration of the University are in Inverness, Perth has more students and many more international students, than any other campus in the University and it hosts the administration of all its international

activities. It brings to Perth large numbers of overseas students and their teachers.

In 2010 Professor Martin Price, the Nobel Peace Laureate from the Mountain Sciences Department of the Perth Campus of the University of the Highlands and Islands brought to Perth **The International Conference on Global Change and the World's Mountains**, which was attended by 450 people from 60 countries. This Conference was preceded by a three-day event bringing together 80 scientists from all over the world for a meeting of the **Global Observation Research Initiate in Alpine Environments**. Perth was indeed exposed to a massive international audience, whose influence in the future can not be measured but should not be underestimated. They, in turn. heard about Perth's ambition to join the ranks of the UK's cities.

Royal Scottish Geographical Society (RSGS). The event that brought a completely new development to Perth and restored and redeveloped Perth's oldest secular building at the same time, was the relocation of the headquarters of the RSGS from

Glasgow to the Fair Maid's House, in Perth. This has significantly increased the academic *critical mass* of Perth. The Society wished to move from cramped rented space in Strathclyde University and purchase a more accessible building which it could develop as the need arose. It has a very extensive archive of maps, books, documents and artefacts, much of it relating to polar exploration. The Society wanted to establish a Scottish centre of excellence for Geography in a building where its collections could be displayed to the public and made available for scholarship and research. It investigated over 50 sites in different locations in Scotland but was finally persuaded to come to Perth. The Society took a long lease on the Fair Maid's House which is owned by the Perth Common Good

Fund and purchased the adjacent Lord John Murray House from Perth & Kinross Council.

The Lord John Murray House, was refurbished fairly quickly and in 2008, was opened as the Society's administrative headquarters by the Princess Royal, who is a Patron of the Society. The adjoining Fair Maid's House, the oldest secular building in Perth, had been empty for a decade and required substantial but sensitive restoration and the addition of a new extension at the back. HRH the Princess Royal visited the RSGS once again in November 2011 to

Lord John Murray's House. Originally the stables of Lord John Murray's town house in Perth. Lord John was the younger son of the first Duke of Atholl, and MP for Perthshire from 1734-1761.

HRH the Princess Royal signing the new visitors' book in the RSGS office at the Lord John Murray House. The text on the facing page reads: *This visitors book started by Her Royal Highness The Princess Royal on Her visit to the new Headquarters of the Royal Scottish Geographical Society in Lord John Murray's House, Perth, on 13th October 2009.*
Image courtesy of the RSGS

The Fair Maid's House. The oldest secular building in Perth. Sir Walter Scott when writing about the events and characters in his novel, *The Fair Maid of Perth*, described the streets and actual buildings in Perth at the time that he wrote the novel. The house features in some of the most dramatic scenes in the book.

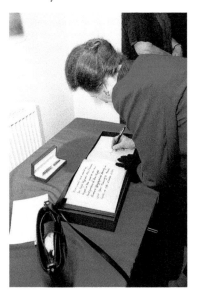

Freshwater Fisheries Research Station in an idyllic situation on the edge of Loch Faskally, near Pitlochry.

The sign post and logo of the James Hutton Institute. Hutton (1726–1797) was a Scottish geologist who first explained how the surface of the earth was formed over deep time by volcanic activity, folding, sedimentation and erosion. He is credited with being the 'Father of modern geology'.

inspected the refurbished buildings and award medals and honorary fellowships on behalf of the Society.

Research Institutes There are two research institutes in Perthshire, both at some distance from Perth itself. *The Freshwater Fisheries Laboratory* on Loch Faskally near Pitlochry is responsible for monitoring and researching the freshwater and migratory fish populations in Scottish waters. Its work is very relevant to the economy of rural Perthshire, where fishing, especially salmon fishing is under threat from many factors, not least climate change.

The other, much larger, research establishment is the *James Hutton Institute* in Invergowrie. This was formed by the union of the Scottish Crop Research Institute at Invergowrie and the Macaulay Land Research institute near Aberdeen. This happened in 2011, just as Perth's city status application was presented to Parliament. It employs more than 500 scientists and support staff, making it one of the biggest research

centres in the UK and the first of its type in Europe. The institute is one of the Scottish Government's main research providers in environmental, crop and food science and will have a major role in the Scottish knowledge economy. Much of the work carried out is closely integrated with Dundee University.

Medical Services
Ensuring that a full range of medical services are available for its population is one of the important functions of a city and regional capital. Since 1914 *Perth Royal Infirmary* has fulfilled this function and has acquired a special place in the hearts of the people of Perthshire. Towards the end of the 1990s, however, the future of the hospital as a District General Hospital, providing a wide range of services, was seriously threatened. To a large extent this was because of the difficulty in attracting junior medical staff to work in what was not a teaching hospital. Ambitious young doctors wanted their CV to record that they had worked in a unit led by a consultant in a Teaching Hospital.

The solution, suggested to Tayside Health Board and the University of Dundee by Perth & Kinross Council in 2000, was to combine the facilities of Perth Royal Infirmary with Ninewells Teaching Hospital and Medical School to form a single entity. The result was a remarkable success, with all the main clinical and teaching units united across the two hospitals and medical, senior nursing and research staff and students, all

circulating between the two. This relieved congestion at Ninewells and provided a local service of the highest quality for patients from Perth & Kinross.

Sadly, in recent years the twin problems that afflict many partnership between organisations of significantly different size (financial pressures and the tendency for the bigger partner to commandeer an ever greater proportion of the mutual resources) have begun to threaten the viability of certain units in PRI once again. Perth's medical community and its democratically elected politicians need to be especially vigilant and pro-active about this matter.

Perth also has a very important role in Scotland's psychiatric services. In 2013 a completely new *Murray Royal* psychiatric hospital was opened on the site of its predecessor. It provides a full range of services to local patients with mental illnesses. However, it also incorporates one of only three Medium Secure Units in Scotland. (The others are in Aberdeen and Glasgow). These specialist units are for prisoners who

have mental illnesses but who are not considered to be a danger to the public. As well as being convenient for patients from Perth & Kinross, the new Murray Royal has secured a substantial number of high quality medical and nursing jobs for Perth.

Conclusion

Throughout the campaign we had sought to raise the profile of Perth in Scotland, in the UK and abroad, so that the Fair City would be noticed in a way that had not happened before. By doing this we hoped to make Perth the subject of 'chatter' among people who might influence the assessment of the claims. As the time for a decision approached, it was clear that the people of Perth at all levels had risen to that challenge and were projecting a confident and enthusiastic image of their city across Scotland and beyond. People, not only in London, were much more aware of Perth and were increasingly receptive to the Perth's claim.

Left

I was surprised and delighted to receive an Honorary Fellowship of the RSGS from HRH the Princess Royal.
Courtesy of the RSGS

Top

The ultramodern Rohallion clinic at the new Murray Royal Hospital. Opinions differ about its architecture.

Above

Perth Royal Infirmary. The notice proudly states 'University Teaching Hospital'.

CHAPTER EIGHT

The second application

Throughout 2010, while the Perth800 celebrations were in full swing, work to promote city status was continuing. Following the refusal of our first application, nothing more was heard from London. The Labour Government and the UK political parties were concentrating on the General Election due in May 2010. After that election the new Conservative/Liberal Democrat Coalition Government took some time to settle down. The Diamond Jubilee celebrations were still two years away and the Civic Honours competition was far from the top priority even in that field. However, one matter that was confirmed soon after the election, was that there would be only one UK winner in the Civic Honour's competition. And so we were under no illusions about the magnitude of the task ahead.

The political hiatus in London gave us an opportunity to re-define our strategy and adjust to the new situation. Baroness Linklater had warned me that almost all parliamentarians and civil servants in London were completely unaware of Perth's history, especially in relation to its status as, *de facto*, the capital of Scotland for 600 years and then its official position as a Royal Burgh and Second City of Scotland until 1975.

While this confirmed what we already suspected, we realised that if

it continued, Perth was unlikely to be treated as a serious contender in the competition and so would probably be an early casualty in any process of elimination. We took some time, therefore to examine Stirling's successful campaign in 2002 and assess the competition from England.

Stirling's Golden Jubilee Campaign

Important factors in Stirling's submission were an excellent, but very expensively produced Claim Document; the emphasis it laid on Stirling's history especially in relation to the castle and the clear demonstration of unanimous support for City Status among its many varied communities.

The other candidate towns

We gleaned what information we could about other towns in England that were preparing for the competition. Among these were several with very strong claims. Some had populations in excess of 200,000 – more than four times the size of Perth. But in many ways the English competitors were so different from Perth, that comparisons were meaningless. It is worth noting, however, that none of those that we considered to be potential winners, was eventually successful.

Milton Keynes was perhaps the largest. From its very foundation as a new town, its officially stated objective was to become a city. Furthermore, it was not far from London and so was familiar to most parliamentarians and civil servants and importantly it was represented by two Conservative MPs.

Reading was the bookies' favourite right from the announcement of the competition. It had twice been unsuccessful in previous competitions and there was much speculation that it would be Reading's turn this time. It had a mixed political background with the Conservative, Labour and Liberal Democrat parties all vying for position.

Medway a conurbation of five boroughs around the Medway estuary in Kent was another strong contender. One of the five towns, Rochester, had been a city from the 13th century and has an ancient cathedral. However, it was demoted (as Perth had been) when it was incorporated into the Medway Unitary Authority as recently as 1998. While Rochester was not a candidate in its own right, the transference of its ancient status to the new Medway Authority was very much part of the Medway campaign.

St William of Perth in Rochester

An interesting indication that news of Perth's endeavours had reached as far south as Kent, came in a letter to me from the Dean of Rochester Cathedral. He wished Perth good luck in the campaign and reminded me that Perth and Rochester were connected through St William of Perth, a 12th century saint, who is buried in Rochester cathedral.

William was born in Perth in about 1165 and was a baxter (baker) to trade. A very devout man, he attended daily Mass. One morning he found an abandoned baby boy on the steps of St John's Kirk. (In the 12th century that was not such an unusual happening). William adopted the baby, who was called David the Foundling.

Some years later, having saved a substantial amount of money, he set out with his son on a pilgrimage to Jerusalem, calling at the main religious destinations on the way. On his way to Canterbury to visit the shrine of Saint Thomas À Becket, he stopped off at Rochester Cathedral. There he was brutally murdered by his adopted son and his purse stolen.

His body was found later by a mad woman, who plaited a garland of honeysuckle and placed it on William's head. Immediately she was cured of her madness. Other miracles followed and in due course he was canonised by Pope Innocent IV and became the patron saint of adopted children.

A shrine in Rochester Cathedral dedicated to his memory, attracted huge numbers of pilgrims, second only to the shrine in Canterbury Cathedral to St Thomas à Becket. Their donations helped to rebuild the cathedral after a disastrous fire and latterly brought considerable wealth to Rochester.

Stained glass window of St William of Perth in Rochester Cathedral. It is remarkable that there is no image, nor indeed any mention of St William, anywhere in Perth.

Priorities for Perth

A careful examination of all the factors enabled us to crystallise our priorities during this period. There were four:

- The most important was to develop Perth's profile among the political élite in London.
- Secondly, we would redouble our efforts to become the leading candidate town from Scotland.
- Thirdly, we would continue to seek to change the 'one winner only' policy and revert to the earlier situation of a winner from each of the constituent nations of the UK.
- Finally we would seek to demonstrate the unanimous and enthusiastic support for Perth's campaign among all sections of the community.

While these were obviously overlapping and complimentary objectives, it was helpful to tease them out into separate strands. Almost all of the activities undertaken by the communities of Perth during the Perth800 celebrations addressed several of these objectives at once.

The Lord Provostship of Perth

A competition for a Lord Mayoralty (Lord Provostship in Scotland) had been announced by Peter Mandelson MP, as part of the Civic Honours competition. The rule was that only cities which had enjoyed official city status for at least 15 years could apply for a Lord Mayoralty/Lord Provostship. In addition, towns which had been elevated to Cities in Civic Honours competitions held to celebrate the Millennium (Inverness in Scotland) and Golden Jubilee (Stirling) were specifically excluded – a completely unnecessary double exclusion. Under this rule there could not be any eligible candidate town in Scotland, which made a mockery of the inclusion of the Lord Provostship in the competition. This amply confirmed Baroness Linklater's assessment of the dismal level of knowledge about Scotland among politicians and civil servants even in the Scottish Office.

Nevertheless, we did consider entering the Lord Provostship competition and emphasising that we were applying for a **restoration** which was not the same as a new application. However caution prevailed and we decided not to enter the competition. Our task was going to be difficult enough without adding complications. The Lord Provostship would have to await another occasion.

A New Team in Westminster

Following the General Election in May 2010, the change to a coalition Government brought forward a new team of politicians. Responsibility for the Diamond Jubilee celebrations moved from the Ministry of Justice to a committee of the Cabinet Office under the chairmanship of the Deputy Prime Minister, Nick Clegg MP, assisted by Mark Harper MP, the Minister of State for Political and Constitutional Reform. Other members of the committee were the Rt Hon Jeremy Hunt MP, Secretary of State for Culture Media and Sport; the Secretaries of State for Scotland (Michael Moore MP), Wales (Cheryl Gillan MP), Northern Ireland (Owen Paterson MP); and for England, Eric Pickles MP, the Secretary of State for Communities and Local Government.

We were pleased that Michael Moore was to be an important member of this group, because he was well known to several of the Liberal Democrat councillors in Perth.

However, even Michael Moore had a lot to learn about Perth's history. In a conversation soon after his appointment, he said that he doubted the validity of Perth's claim for the **restoration** of its city status saying he was unaware of any evidence that Perth had actually ever been a city. It was the tired old story of, 'No Royal Declaration, No Letters Patent, No Charter or other document; therefore not a city'. Of course he had not considered whether these criteria also applied to Edinburgh or Glasgow and if they did, why there was no doubt about their status. I had to draw his attention to the historical evidence outlined in some detail in Chapter 3 and I sent him a copy of our first City Status Claim document. Thereafter he proved to be a stalwart friend of Perth, especially after Perth was confirmed as the only candidate town from Scotland.

Application criteria

In due course the criteria for the competition were published. Contrary to the previous competitions, when specific guidelines were given, the main priority on this occasion was to simplify the assessment process and limit the cost to the Local Authorities. The application, which had to come from a Local Authority, was to consist of a single A4 document, comprising no more than 25 pages of text and 50 photographs, printed two to a page. Two maps were required, one showing the candidate town within its local area and the other a map of the town itself. In the event, Perth's document consisted of 25 pages of text and 48 photographs, including those on the front cover and on the inside of the front cover. The document was to be submitted by 4.00pm on Friday 27 May 2011.

While the Government offered no guidance about what should or should not be included by candidate towns in their claim documents, we took care to study the requirements that had been published for the competitions in 2000 and 2002. The over-arching priority was that the town should be the commercial and administrative centre of a large area and be the hub for all the important public services, including especially health and education. It should also be the main centre for retail, leisure and sports facilities for its area.

We were also aware that Royal and military connections were important, as was a good record of local government and financial management.

The Application Document

Meanwhile, back at the Council HQ in 2 High Street, work was proceeding on our second application document. The contents had to condense the work of four years into fewer than 10,000 words of text, complimented by appropriate quotations and illustrations. It was essential to refer, either in the text, the illustrations, or the quotations, to every important element of Perth's claim:

- History: Previous capital and official second city;
- The geo-political centrality of Perth within Scotland and within its county;
- Royal and military connections;
- Commercial success;
- The new University and other academic institutions;
- Arts and literature;
- Sport;
- A competent, ably led Council providing excellent public services;
- The environment;
- And finally the universality of support for Perth's ambition from within its own community and also from across Scotland and beyond.

There was not the haste that there had been at the time of the first application, allowing time to write the document and design what we were told was by far the best of all the competition entries.

Not for Perth the pedestrian

appearance of 25 pages of text, followed by 50 pictures arranged like postcards, pasted two to a page in a photograph album. In Perth's document the images varied in size and shape – some large and square, others round, some standing alone and others overlapping. They were carefully selected to complement the text on the facing page and then skilfully cropped and placed with a graphic designer's eye, alongside informative legends and quotations from our advocates. It was this design flair that made Perth's document unique among the entries.

The front cover set the scene. The main picture featured some spectacular fireworks over Perth, lighting up the public face of Perth – the river, Tay Street and the silhouettes of St Matthew's Church and the dome of the Council building. The smaller picture was a photograph showing 700 primary school children spelling out

The larger of the two images that graced the front cover of Perth's Application for City Status.
© Mike Brunton, (Perthshire Photographic Society)

Perth

800

on the North Inch. Euna Scott, who was the driving force behind Perth's successful involvement in the 'Bloom' competitions, arranged for a photographer to be taken up Tayside Fire Brigade's tallest ladder to capture the image. The whole cover exuded *joie de vivre*, confidence, commitment and excitement.

The picture inside the front cover hammered home the message that Perth was Scotland's candidate for City Status and that it was supported across the nation. It showed the leaders of Scotland's four main political parties coming together to sign the support document. (See picture, p. 145).

The second picture on this page was of the Coat of Arms of Perth & Kinross Council. The legend alongside explained that the Double Headed Eagle bearer is one of the oldest heraldic symbols in the world, dating back 5000 years to the Sumerian city of Lagash in Mesopotamia.

The text on the facing page included a quotation from Alex Salmond: 'I'm fully supporting the campaign for City Status for the Royal Burgh of Perth'.

The next page dealt with the 'Historical Basis for Perth's Claim for City Status'. It noted the main issues covered in Chapter 2 of this book and included the following quotation from Professor AAM Duncan,

> In the 12th century, Perth was the second town in

'Perth800' spelled out by 700 primary school children on the North Inch, and captured by a photographer high up on a Fire Brigade ladder. The picture was the smaller of the two images on the front cover of the Claim Document.
Courtesy of The *Courier*
© DCThomson.co.uk

Scotland: second that is to Berwick-upon-Tweed and far ahead of Edinburgh, Aberdeen or Stirling in importance.[1]

It carried a photograph of the King William Charter of 1210 and the replica Stone of Destiny which is outside Scone Palace. The text outlined in brief the main elements of the history of these two important artefacts.

An important page focussed on Perth's military connections and featured the impressive photograph by Graeme Hart of Prince Edward taking the salute by 3SCOTS, (See picture, p. 87) during the Perth Day parade. Other pages featured Perth's important businesses; its emphasis on art and culture, sport, education and academia, its plethora of cafés, its famous sons, its matchless environment and, of course, its well led Council.

---

1 Prof. AAM Duncan, 'Perth, the First Century of the Burgh' 1974

Perth's Boundaries

The requirement to produce a map showing the boundaries of the proposed new city may have been included to forestall an anomaly like the City of Carlisle, which is the largest city by area in England. It covers over 400 square miles, most of it sparsely populated sheep farms and moorland. (For comparison Durham has an area of 72 Square miles). However, it triggered a consideration of what the boundaries of a new City of Perth should be.

Perth's boundaries were defined when local government was reorganised in 1996, The need to submit a map for the competition provided an opportunity to reconsider them in the light of current realities and the potential for the future expansion of the city. It was decided therefore to add two new areas to the proposed city. The first was an area to the north and east of Perth, encompassing Scone and Kinfauns. Scone is a large village less than a mile north of the existing urban boundary of Perth across the green belt. Although now very much a commuter suburb, it was once a royal burgh in its own right and had very strong historical connections with Perth. Nowadays it certainly has a 'Perth feel' about it. Kinfauns is a village at the western end of the Carse of Gowrie and includes a modest amount of housing and the site for a future 'park and ride' facility.

The second area was to the northwest of Perth, on both banks of the River Almond, including Bertha Park (the site of a proposed major expansion of Perth} and the villages of Almondbank and Pitcairn Green. These changes had the effect of increasing the official population of Perth from 45,000 to just over 50,000. We considered this to be a significant threshold at a time when it seemed that Perth might suffer discrimination because of its relatively small size. However, the changes were probably irrelevant, and have made no difference to the governance of Perth since.

The Final Act

Pete Wishart MP and I personally delivered two copies of the document to the Cabinet Office in Westminster on 25 May, two days before the deadline, taking care to ensure that our visit was covered by Westminster based reporters and photographers as well as the press from Perth.

With Pete Wishart MP at the Cabinet Office to deliver two copies of the claim document on the 25 May 2011.

CHAPTER NINE

Unexpected Government 'U' Turn

By the autumn of 2010 we were aware of 11 candidate towns in England, two in Wales and one in Northern Ireland, but no others from Scotland. And so I wrote to the Provosts and Council leaders of Dumfries and Galloway, South Ayrshire, Renfrewshire, Fife and Moray to ascertain whether there were any plans for Dumfries, Ayr, Paisley, Dunfermline or Elgin to enter the campaign. There was none.

The fact that Perth was to be the only candidate for City Status from Scotland was a severe setback. It put at naught our strategy which had been to win the Scottish element of a Civic Honours competition which we assumed would take place in each of the four nations of the UK. Instead we found we were engaged in a much wider, more daunting competition involving Wales and Northern Ireland as well as England, from which only one winner could emerge. However, it did also mean that we could lobby for support from all of Scotland and from all the political parties and become in effect Scotland's candidate in the UK competition. Politicians and others who were wary about siding with one Scottish town against another, were happy to support a single Scottish candidate.

Civic Leaders

We already had good relations with the Lord Provosts and Provosts of Scotland's six existing cities, all of whom had attended events in Perth during the Homecoming or Perth800 celebrations. Indeed, the Lord Provosts of Dundee and Edinburgh and the Provosts of Stirling and Angus had been quite frequent visitors. I invited them to endorse our application, which they all did. Quotations, including the two below, were selected from these endorsements and used in the Claim Document.

> Perth is an intrinsic part of our Scottish history, as well as being a forward thinking, successful and dynamic place to be. I am honoured to lend my support to the Royal Burgh of Perth's application to have its ancient title of City Status restored.
>
> Rt Hon George Grubb, Lord Lieutenant and Lord Provost of Edinburgh.
>
> Dundee will be fully supportive in any way we can to ensure your deserved success, so you can indeed depend our friendship and

determination to help your cause.

John Letford, Lord Lieutenant and Lord Provost of Dundee.

Holyrood

On 25 February 2010 Murdo Fraser, a Conservative List MSP for Mid Scotland and Fife, who lives in Perth, introduced a debate in the Scottish Parliament congratulating Perth on the programme for its 800th anniversary celebrations and supporting the campaign to restore its historic City Status. During the debate MSPs from across Scotland and from all the political parties spoke in support of Perth. John Swinney, the MSP for Perthshire North and the Cabinet Secretary for Finance and Sustainable Growth, concluded the debate. He added the Scottish Government's congratulations for the Homecoming and Perth800 programmes and said that these celebrations had created a wonderful springboard from which to launch the campaign for official City Status.

I went with a delegation from the Council to listen to the debate and after it we mounted a small exhibition outside the chamber, illustrating some of the Perth800 events and making available our first City Status claim document to those who were interested and wanted a copy. We also had forms, 'Supporting Perth's Bid to Restore its City Status' and many of the MSPs signed them.

Following the debate I wrote to all the MSPs who had contributed and thanked them for their efforts. I reminded them that the decision would be made in London and I asked them to keep up the pressure for Perth on their fellow parliamentarians in London.

House of Commons

As noted on page 68, just before our Westminster Dinner on 7 December 2009, a cross Party group of MPs led by Pete Wishart MP and including Gordon Banks MP (Labour), Michael Fallon MP (Conservative), Lord John Thurso MP (Liberal Democrat) tabled an Early Day Motion. This congratulated Perth on the planned celebrations and looked forward to Perth becoming Scotland's seventh city.

Almost exactly a year later, on 16 December 2010, Mr Wishart secured a debate in the House of commons on the Government's plans for the Civic Honours competition. He used the occasion to question the proposal to award recognition to only one city in the UK. He also highlighted what he called, 'Perth's compelling case' for City Status.

On every occasion, in every location – Perth, Edinburgh, London – Perth's case was being made.

The contestants

In London, throughout the latter part of 2010, the competition was hotting up with new candidate towns being announced regularly. By the close of applications on 27 May 2011, 26 towns had applied for city status. They were Bolton, Bournemouth,

Chelmsford, Colchester, Coleraine, Corby, Craigavon, Croydon, Doncaster, Dorchester, Dudley, Gateshead, Goole, Luton, Medway, Middlesbrough, Milton Keynes, Perth, Reading, Southend, St Asaph, St Austell, Stockport, Tower Hamlets and Wrexham.

Twelve established cities had applied for a Lord Mayoralty. They were: Armagh, Cambridge, Derby, Gloucester, Lancaster, Newport, Peterborough, Salford, Southampton, St Albans, Sunderland and Wakefield. There was none of course from Scotland.

Surprisingly, the Prime Minister, David Cameron, came out publicly in favour of Reading, which quickly became the bookies' favourite. It continued to hold that top position right up to the declaration of the result. Perth's position in the gambling stakes was consistently three or four places behind Reading. Even that was remarkable considering Perth's size, its remoteness from London and its political representation. Notwithstanding this relatively good position, it seemed most unlikely that a small Scottish town could ever be the only winner from the UK. It was essential to secure a change in this rule.

Government 'U' turn brings first hint of success

The First Minister, Alex Salmond, was a redoubtable supporter of Perth as Scotland's candidate. He, of course, had regular meetings with David Cameron and I was made aware on a couple of occasions that he had raised Perth's aspirations for city status. In February 2011, therefore, I wrote to the Prime Minister as a follow up to one of his discussions with the First Minister pointing out that Perth was alone in seeking **restoration** of City Status. I also highlighted Scotland's unique relationship with the Royal Family, which, I suggested, might be damaged if a town from England was the only winner.

The reply I received on the 24 May 2011 from Mark Harper, MP, the Minister for Political and Constitutional Reform, was our first success and it beamed a ray of real hope into the Council Headquarters in Perth. He said that if there were entries of sufficient calibre it was 'possible for the Civic Honours competition to result in more than one winner'.

With the possibility of more than one winner in the competition, we had achieved our most important strategic objective.

CHAPTER TEN

The Final Push

With the claim document submitted, the waiting began. No one knew when the decision would be announced, but it seemed unlikely that it would be before the beginning of 2012, the Jubilee Year. The most likely dates were:

- The New Year, at the same time as the New Year Honours list.
- February 6, which was the 60th anniversary of the death of King George VI and the Queen's legal accession to the throne;
- Early in June when the official Jubilee celebrations were due to take place.

A problem with a June date was that local elections were due in May in many of the competing towns and cities, including Perth. The resulting political changes would sever the continuity between the claim process and the result, which would be unfortunate.

No matter which date was chosen, I was quite sure that after they were lodged, the applications would have been locked away safely with no more than a cursory inspection. Then when the date was imminent, they would be brought out, examined and a decision made. This fallow period

in relation to Civic Honours was exactly the time when our advocates could be most useful, promoting Perth in a low key, non-controversial manner.

Advocates for Perth

In preparation for this, we stepped up the search for Advocates who were likely to have the right contacts in London (See p. 59). Since Perth was now Scotland's only representative in the competition, it was no longer necessary for all of our advocates to have a strong Perth connection. It was, however, very important to recruit advocates with a wide range of backgrounds in order to tap into the different strands of advice that would be directed towards those who would make the decision about City Status.

Politicians

Most, perhaps even all, of Scotland's elected politicians were on Perth's side, including the First Minister, Alex Salmond, Nicola Sturgeon, the Deputy First Minister and Minister for Cities and the Secretary of State for Scotland, Michael Moore, all of whom made no secret of their lobbying on our behalf. All of Scotland's six MEPs supported Perth, as did many of the

Westminster MPs and some members of the House of Lords.

One retired politician whom I approached early in 2011 was the Rt Hon George Reid, (now Sir George Reid) a former MP and MSP and perhaps the most highly regarded Scottish politician of his generation. As Presiding Officer of the Scottish Parliament from 2003 to 2007 and a Privy Councillor, he had a duty to advise HM the Queen about Scottish matters. Since he retired from Parliament in 2007, he had had a number of high profile Royal appointments including that of Lord High Commissioner to the General Assembly of the Church of Scotland. I knew him as a fellow Parliamentary candidate in the 1970s and we had met occasionally since. We were both invited to a reception in Edinburgh hosted by the Russian Consul General and so I took the opportunity to tell him of Perth's ambition. He was delighted to accept the role of Advocate for Perth. During our conversation he assured me that the Queen would play a very important role in the decision about City Status.

The Media

We had a powerful group from the media who supported our campaign. The local newspapers, the Courier and the Perthshire Advertiser, were thoroughly committed and we had support from the Scottish broadsheets and from Magnus Linklater, the Scottish editor of the Times and husband of Baroness Linklater. On National TV, Gordon MacMillan, Head of News at STV

was an advocate and we had some individual supporters from the BBC, including Perth born Stuart Cosgrove and Fred MacAulay. Reporters form the local STV station based in Dundee attended a fair number of Perth800 and City Status events, but the BBCTV ignored Perth.

Academics

We had support from Professor Martin Price, the Nobel Peace Prize laureate and Director of the Centre for Mountain Studies at the Perth campus of the University the Highlands and Islands. Other academics among our Advocates were the Principal of Perth College, Dr Thomas Moore, his immediate predecessor, Ms Mandy Exley and Professor Peter Gregory who was the Director and Chief Executive of the Scottish Crop Research Institute in Invergowrie (now the James Hutton Institute).

Civic, Business and Military Leaders

This was the most disparate group of advocates, collectively reaching out to the institutions of the British State that were impervious to the entreaties of politicians and Local Authorities. One of them was John Vine, former Chief Constable of Tayside, who was appointed Her Majesty's Chief Inspector of Borders and Immigration in 2009. His duties in London brought him into contact with many senior politicians and civil servants and his continuing family connections with Perthshire provided him with opportunities to mention Perth.

Also based locally was the Mansfield family from Scone Palace. Their connection with Perth extends back to 1600, when they were granted Scone Palace and its estate by James VI. In recent decades they have been much involved in business, tourism and social work in Perth. Moreover they are close to the Royal Family, in particular to Prince Charles.

Our main request was that our advocates facilitate a regular flow of positive information about Perth and our city status ambition. One who would be able to do this in the West of Scotland, where Perth's ambition was relatively unknown, was Lord MacFarlane of Bearsden, the honorary life president of Diageo, whose whisky interests included the former iconic Perth companies of Bells and Dewars.

Some of our advocates had unlikely backgrounds. One such was Roger Gifford, an Alderman in the City of London, who owned a holiday property in Perthshire.

Perth's connections with the Black Watch and through the Lord Lieutenant with the Royal Scots Dragoon Guards, enabled us to recruit some high ranking military men, including Lt General Sir Alastair Irwin who was the chairman of the Black Watch Museum Trust.

Other support

In addition to those who had agreed to become Advocates, there were a number of individuals who were aware of Perth's aspirations and whom we judged were very likely to support our claim, but who were debarred by their office from making public any formal or even informal commitment on behalf of Perth. These included members of the Royal Household, some of whom had visited Perth during our Perth800 celebrations and politicians with positions in the Government at Westminster, I did not court refusal by asking them to become advocates, but we sent them occasional informal updates about Perth, including especially, information about the City Status developments, in the hope (and indeed expectation) that they might contribute in a non-controversial way to the 'positive chatter' about Perth.

Community support

Throughout the second half of 2010 and into 2011 we developed this twin track strategy to build general support for Perth locally and across Scotland while we pursued individuals with influence in London.

We made a great effort to

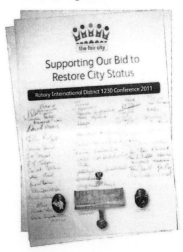

Several sheets of supporting signatures from the Rotary International District 1230 Conference. 2011.

demonstrate to the media and to opinion formers in London that support for Perth's claim was practically universal locally, but was also strong among all the communities of Scotland, especially so since it became clear that Perth was to be the only Scottish candidate. Forms pledging support for City Status for Perth were made available in libraries and other public buildings for people to sign. I made it my business to take them to the many events that I attended, where they were signed by local people and by visitors from every part of Scotland and from England and abroad.

A high profile event in the Holyrood Parliament building demonstrated the strength of support for Perth among Scotland's politicians. Just a few days before the Scottish Parliament was dissolved prior to the election in 2011, we managed to persuade the leaders of Scotland's four major parties – Alex Salmond for the SNP, Iain Gray for Labour, Annabel Goldie for the Conservatives and Tavish Scott for the Liberal Democrats – to sink their differences and come together for a joint signing of our support document in front of the Press.

It was done with a flourish, to the sound of the bagpipes of Perth's City Piper proclaiming that something important was happening. There was a steady stream of MSPs passing by, many of whom were curious as to what could possibly bring the four leaders and a piper together at such a time. When they came over to investigate, many signed our

document. While they could hardly be considered to be Advocates, the support from so many parliamentarians and the interest that they would undoubtedly generate, was very important. Perth was certainly getting noticed.

First Minister, Alex Salmond, signs Perth's Support document, to be followed by Ian Gray, Annabel Goldie, and Tavish Scott, watched by Perth's City piper, Alastair Duthie.
© Angus Findlay. This picture appeared on the inside front cover of our claim document (see p. 137)

Business Support

Support from local businesses was also very important. Bidwells, the property consultants, hosted a special reception at a critical stage in the Autumn of 2011, at which all of Perth's businesses, large and small, were invited to sign the campaign sponsorship document. We judged

Gilbert Strang of the Perth based company Bidwells, signs the support document at the Business reception.

that it was very important to emphasise the solidarity of the Perth community behind the City Status bid and this reception allowed the business sector *en masse* to register its support as businesses, rather than the various businessmen signing as individuals.

Supporting document

By the Autumn of 2011 the level of public support had reached tsunami proportions and we sought a way of communicating this to the competition judges. We were advised in October that evidence to back up our competition entry (which had been submitted in May) would be accepted up to the middle of November.

To take full advantage of this unexpected opportunity, the responses we had received were collated and a selection of them copied and bound. We took trouble to ensure that the responses included came from a very wide cross section of the population of Perth and from elsewhere in Scotland, the rest of the UK and Europe.

Endorsements

I asked our advocates to write a short paragraph about City Status, which might be used in our campaign. Many of those we received were very powerful statements indeed. Some were used in the Application document and others in the Supporting Document. Three are quoted here.

For as long as I can remember Perth has been referred to as 'The Fair City', a title which it thoroughly deserves. As a member of the extended Black Watch family, I emphasise that Perth was and remains, the home of the British Army's most famous regiment. The Black Watch is proud of its association with Perth and believes that it would be more than fitting that city status should be granted. I lend my wholehearted support to the bid and wish it every success.

LT GENERAL SIR ALASTAIR IRWIN KCB, CBE, Chairman, The Black Watch Museum Trust

The Mansfield family are immensely proud of their 600+ years connection with the City of Perth, as it is yet known. Perth deserves to be given back its legal right to this title for historic, cultural and commercial reasons.

LADY PAMELA, Countess of Mansfield

Perth is Scotland's First city and should never have lost its City Status. As the Gateway to the Highlands and the centre of Scotland's first Parliament, Perth is the outstanding candidate for city Status.

MICHAEL FALLON MP

A particularly trenchant comment was received from the Right Honourable Sir David Edward, KCMG, QC, LLD, FRSE, former Judge of the European Court of Justice and Professor Emeritus of Edinburgh University. It is reproduced in full below and an excerpt appeared on the front cover of the Support Document.

> I was born and brought up in Perth and I received my early education at Perth Academy. As far as I know, all my forebears on both sides of my family were born not more than 50 miles from Perth, with the exception of my mother who was born in Sussex, where my grandfather had gone to learn the modern techniques of road construction. He returned to be Road Surveyor of the eastern district of Perthshire.

> My great grandfather on my father's side was a warder in Perth Prison and latterly the City Chamberlain's personal officer. My father followed my grandfather as a travel agent and house factor in County Place. My grandfather collected church communion tokens and gave his magnificent collection to Perth Museum.

> So I believe I can claim to be a true son of Perth and was proud to serve as an Honorary Sheriff.

> I was brought up to be conscious of Perth's history and ancient civic status. Successive Lord Provosts were knighted and were significant figures in Scottish public life. The loss of Perth's status as a city, was for me, an act of bureaucratic vandalism. So I most fervently support the campaign to restore Perth's ancient and honourable title.

This document was submitted in November 2011. After that, there was nothing to do but wait.

CHAPTER ELEVEN

City Status Achieved: The Announcement, The Celebrations and The Award

The Announcement

Right up until Monday 12 March, there had been no indication as to when the results of the Civic Honours competition would be announced. I had hoped it might be made at the time of the release of the New Year Honours list, or on 6 February, the date of the Queen's accession. But these deadlines passed without any mention of the competition. I was beginning to fear that it would not happen until the Jubilee weekend at the beginning of June, after I had demitted office at the Council elections.

However, on 12 March, the Lord Lieutenant received a phone call from one of the Palace secretaries in London, telling him that there would be an announcement on the following Wednesday – but no indication of which way that announcement would go. Then on Tuesday things began to happen. Pete Wishart MP phoned me twice from London first of all saying that the announcement was definitely going to be made the next day and then, a little later, to report that there was an avalanche of rumours suggesting that

Perth was going to be successful for Scotland and Reading for England.

In the afternoon David Mundell, MP, the Under Secretary of State for Scotland, phoned me, but I was out. He phoned my home again in the evening at about 8.00pm and asked if he could come to my office in Perth the next morning, at 9.15. He told me that an order would be laid before Parliament at 9.30 the next morning announcing the result of the Civic Honours competition. I asked if Perth had been successful. He said that while he did not want to end up in the Tower of London for leaking information, he thought that I could be optimistic about the result!

The meeting with David Mundell MP was arranged and a press conference organised for ten o'clock in the Civic Lounge. Two press releases were prepared – one to be used if we were successful and the other if we were not.

The Courier, through its contacts in London, also got wind of the developments and phoned me. I let them know what David Mundell had said and that he had asked to come and see me in the morning. That was enough for *The Courier* and the

editor decided to jump the gun and he printed the story that hit Perth's streets early on Wednesday morning with the headline 'It's Perth City', many hours before the actual announcement.

While *The Courier* got the scoop a day early, other papers followed on the Thursday and even *The Times* reported it on its front page.

That day (Wednesday 14th) saw Perth, Cheltenham and St Asaph winning city status, but not Reading. And so the avalanche of rumours was only half correct and Reading and some other English towns were bitterly disappointed. Armagh in Northern Ireland was granted a Lord Mayoralty.

At the press conference there were speeches from Brigadier Jameson, the Lord Lieutenant, Cllr Ian Miller, the Leader of the Council, David Mundell MP, the Under Secretary of State for Scotland and myself.

In my speech I reflected on Perth's history from mediaeval to modern times and the history of the City

Status campaign. I noted in particular that Perth's campaign almost certainly saved the Civic Honours competition at the time when the Labour Government in Westminster planned to scrap it. I also said that the strong support that Perth received from all across Scotland, probably ensured that not only Scotland, but also Northern Ireland, Wales and indeed England all ended up with winners. I firmly believe that without Perth's campaign, none of this would have happened. Perth deserved credit for this from across the UK.

After the Press Conference we all went down to the promontory overlooking the Tay for a photo-shoot. We opened a couple of bottles of champagne, although some of us were careful not to actually drink it at the time, lest we be arrested for flouting the Council's by-law about drinking alcohol in public places!

It was a very exciting and rewarding day.

A Summer of events and celebrations

There followed nearly four months of waiting until the visit of HM The

The front page of *The Courier*, on 14 March, published several hours before the announcement.
Image courtesy of *The Courier*.
© DC Thomson & Co. Ltd.

The Times, and several other London papers reported Perth's success on the front page.

Celebrating with the Lord Lieutenant on the Promontory overlooking the Tay.
Courtesy of the *Perthshire Advertiser*

3SCOTS Homecoming Parade, 2012.
© Angus Findlay

Queen and the presentation of the Letters Patent and at last the official restoration of City Status. But they were not dreary empty months – they were filled with activities and events, almost as if the campaign was continuing.

3SCOTS – Second Homecoming

Shortly after the City Status announcement there was a second homecoming parade for 3SCOTS, the Black Watch Battalion. During the Iraq War and the Afghanistan

Lt Colonel Fenton addresses the gathering at the reception in the Concert Hall Foyer after the parade.
© Angus Findlay

Perth and Kinross Welcomes

The Black Watch, 3rd Battalion The Royal Regiment of Scotland

&

Veterans of The Black Watch, Royal Highland Regimen

conflict, units such as 3SCOTS did a six month tour of Duty in the war zone every three or four years. In December 2009, I was privileged to welcome the Battalion back from their first tour of Afghanistan (they had been to Iraq previously). On this occasion I welcomed them back from a second tour. It had been a very different tour this time. The major battles against the Taliban had all been won, but the guerrilla war continued. This time the Battalion's duties had consisted mostly of policing the area and training the Afghan soldiers. It was not without risk from renegade Afghan soldiers or from roadside bombs, but although there were some very serious injuries, there had not been any fatalities.

Signed model of the statue of the Fair Maid of Perth by Graham Ibbeson, given to me at the last Council meeting. The Council commissioned the miniatures of the statue in the High Street, to use as official gifts for the mayors of our twin cities.

The Reception

After such a long campaign involving so many people, it was appropriate to have some kind of official celebration. With the Council elections imminent and several of those involved retiring, it was right and proper that such an event should be held by the outgoing Council which had initiated, planned and executed the entire campaign, rather than hold it over until the official recognition and presentation of the Letters Patent by the Queen took place in July. It was also very important to have an early opportunity to thank all of those who had contributed to its success.

And so a reception in the Concert Hall foyer was held on the evening of the 25 April, to which everyone who had been connected with the campaign was invited. The last Council meeting had been convened in the afternoon of that day. It was my last meeting in the chair, at which I was delighted to be presented with a signed model of Graham Ibbeson's statue of the Fair Maid sitting on her bench in the High Street. I used the opportunity of that meeting to thank the councillors and council staff who had facilitated the campaign by their enthusiasm and hard work. The reception in the evening was for the people of Perth and of the wider community of Scotland.

It was a very large reception attended by a broad cross section of those who had been involved through sports clubs, arts organisations and community groups. The Lord Lieutenant of Perth & Kinross was there as well as councillors, council officers, members of the local

Four of the five Provosts at the reception. Provost Jimmy Gray of Inverness (left), Lord Provosts Peter Stephen of Aberdeen (centre left), and Lord Provost John Letford 0f Dundee (right).
Image courtesy of *The Courier*
© DC Thomson & Co. Ltd

We were entertained by Perth's unique Jamboree choir, led by Edna Auld.

For many of us that evening, there were genuine feelings of climax and anticlimax – climax at having prevailed against the very considerable odds that were stacked against Perth in 2007; anticlimax because of the knowledge that in seven short days, our Council would be dissolved and a new chapter in Perth's history opened. Personally, however, I was consoled by the knowledge that Perth's status as a City of Scotland was now unchallenged.

The Council Election

The Council elections were held on 3 May, just a week after the reception. While they caused major political shocks in many Councils across Scotland, in Perth there was little change in the overall Party balance, although, of course there were several new faces. I had retired after 17 years as a Councillor and five as the Provost. I left the Provostship with mixed emotions. There was elation at the success of the City Status campaign, but sadness that we had not achieved the restoration of the Lord Provostship.

The election was followed in rapid order by the Diamond Jubilee Celebrations on the weekend of 1st to 3rd June and then the visit of Her Majesty the Queen on the 7 July. Preparations for both these events had long predated the announcement of the results on the 14 March and had been treated as if they were extensions of the Civic Honours campaign.

judiciary, church ministers and others.

A very pleasant surprise was the number of distinguished and very busy people from outwith Perth who thought it appropriate to give up an evening to come to Perth and celebrate with us. They included members of both Houses of Parliament, some senior military officers, the Consuls General of Germany, France and Poland, the Lord Provosts of Aberdeen and Dundee and the Provosts of Inverness and Stirling. Importantly a number of our distinguished advocates, including Lord Gill and Sir David Edward, also attended. I sincerely believed that our advocates had been crucial to the success of the campaign and I was delighted that so many of them chose to come. The fact that they did so suggested to me that they had indeed lobbied discretely for Perth and were keen to share in the success to which they had contributed.

Diamond Jubilee Weekend

Whatever the outcome of the City Status campaign, Perth had planned to mark the Diamond Jubilee with a major three-day celebration, to which the mayors of all our twin cities had been invited. Perth's reputation for staging spectacular parades and other events was well known to the citizens of our twin towns and so a considerable number of them came to take part in the festivities, especially from Aschaffenburg. Once again the German contingent included a section of the Spessart Highlanders Pipe Band, who were due to take part in the Parade of 1,000 pipers on the Saturday. In honour of that band's long relationship with The Perth & District, The Blairgowrie and The Vale of Atholl Pipe Bands, the Pipe Major was presented with a Pipe Banner to be carried at all important occasions.

While the Jubilee celebrations would have gone ahead whatever the result of the Civic Honours competition, in the new circumstances there was a spirit of sheer elation which pervaded everything that happened during that weekend.

Pillar Sculptures

During civic visits to our twin cities, I had noticed that several of them had celebrated their links with Perth in strong physical terms. As noted on page 45 Aschaffenburg had named a river-side walk Perth Inch and erected a stone sculpture alongside. Pskov also had memorial stones erected adjacent to a riverside walk (see p. 46). Cognac celebrated its link to Perth by naming a prominent street Rue de Perth. Perth had no comparable civic commemoration.[1]

The Lady Provost suggested that a suitable public art commemoration of Perth's twinning links in the Perth800 year would be to carve the coats of arms of our twin cities onto blank pillars on the Tay Street flood wall.

The most visible section of Perth's award winning flood defences is the four foot high flood wall along Tay Street, between the Perth Bridge and the Railway Bridge. The monotony of such a long wall is relieved and the wall itself strengthened, by 35 square sandstone pillars, topped with pyramidal caps in late Georgian style. Fifteen of these pillars were decorated by panels sculpted by the local artist Gillian Forbes when the defences were built in 2001. The carvings feature icons of Perth's history, its fauna and flora, people and places and some are incised with verses from the poems of William Soutar, Perth's most famous literary son.

The suggestion to use five of the blank pillars to commemorate our twin cities was readily approved and in due course Gillian Forbes was again commissioned to carry out the work. The pillars chosen were

---

1 Aschaffenburg is commemorated in the St John's Centre. The German city's coat of arms appears above the High Street entrance to the Centre and St Martyn's House, the offices above the Centre are named after Aschaffenburg's patron saint.

whenever the mayor next visited Perth. The first one to do so was Michel Gourinchas, the Mayor of Cognac, who came with a party of *Les Amis de Perth*, in April 2011 to celebrate the 20th anniversary of the Cognac Twinning. There were no other mayoral visits until the Jubilee celebrations and so the remaining four sculptures were unveiled by the respective mayors during the Jubilee weekend.

Parade of 1,000 Pipers

The Jubilee weekend coincided with Armed Forces Day, which Perth always celebrates in style. On this occasion we planned a parade of 1,000 pipers and drummers – the biggest such parade in Scotland. To muster 1,000 musicians, especially on Armed Forces Day, when many other towns were planning similar parades, required major organisation. All of Perthshire's local bands were involved of course, but we also attracted district bands from Fife, Angus and Stirlingshire, British Legion bands and Army Cadet bands from all over Scotland, the Spessart Highlanders from Aschaffenburg and many individual pipers.

Normally such an important parade would have been led by the pipes and drums of the Black Watch (3SCOTS), but following its Homecoming Parade, that battalion was on well deserved leave. And so the parade was led by the pipe band from 4SCOTS, the Highlander Battalion of the Royal Regiment of

allocated according to the seniority of the twinning link. The first blank pillar, when walking downstream from the Perth Bridge, was for Aschaffenburg, then Cognac, Pskov (after the promontory), then Bydgoszcz and finally Perth (Ontario). Haikou, in China, does not have a coat of arms or an armorial crest and so, sadly, there is no pillar sculpture for our Chinese twin city.

The plan was to have an unveiling ceremony for each of the twin cities

Above left

Coat of Arms of Aschaffenburg, featuring St Martyn, its Patron Saint. Twinned with the City of Perth 1956.

Above middle

The Coat of Arms of Bydgoszcz, showing the gates of the city, opened. Twinned with the City of Perth 1998.

Above right

The Lamb of St John with staff and banner from Perth Ontario. Twinned with the City of Perth 2001.

Middle left

Ville de Cognac. The coat of arms of the French city of Cognac, with three Fleurs de Lys, and a mounted knight. Twinned with the City of Perth, 1991.

Left

The Snow Leopard of Pskov. Twinned with the City of Perth 1991.

Scotland. Many of the bands came with their colours and these were grouped together and made a colourful spectacle. Finally, bringing up the rear was the Famous Grouse mascot. The weather was kind and the parade was a great success.

The Kilt Run

During the civic visit to Perth (Ontario) in 2010, the Canadians held an 8km Kilt Run in honour of the 800th anniversary of their mother town of Perth in Scotland (1km for every 100 years). The only qualification for entry was that a kilt had to be worn. It was a fun race, completed in temperatures of over 30°C, with many whole families running together. In all, 1089 competitors completed the race and I was honoured to be asked to present the prizes. After the prize giving, the Mayor of Perth, Ontario, Mr John Fenik (who himself had taken part in the race), issued a challenge to Perth, Scotland. He asked us to stage our own Kilt Run

Above

The big drums of 4SCOTS the Highlander Battalion of the Royal Regiment of Scotland.
© Angus Findlay

Middle

The colour parties of the various cadet companies participating were grouped together.
© Angus Findlay

Left

Over 1000 runners approach the starting line of the Kilt Run in Perth Ontario.

A group of runners accompany Gilbert, the Famous Grouse mascot on Perth's Kilt run.
© Angus Findlay

and surpass that number of competitors before 2016 – the date of the 200th anniversary of the founding of Perth Ontario (for which big celebrations were already being planned). In my speech I accepted the challenge and at the Jubilee weekend it was put to the test. In the event Perth (Scotland) managed just over 1,000 competitors in the Jubilee Kilt Run, just missing out on beating the target. Perhaps next time.

Kirking of the Council and the Garden Party on 3 June

The Kirking is the annual church service to rededicate the Council to the service of the people of Perth & Kinross. It is held in late May or early June and it is a particularly special event when it occurs immediately after a Council election, as in 2012. And so it was very appropriate that the twinning mayors were present on this occasion and were able to appreciate the solemnity of the occasion in the ancient High Kirk of St John's of Perth.

In the afternoon the twinning delegations came to our house in

Informal garden party for the twinning delegations, with my family and even our black labrador.

Longforgan for an informal garden party. By that time I was, of course, no longer the provost, nor indeed a councillor, so the farewells to the mayors, some of whom I had got to know very well over the previous five years, were unofficial, but no less sincere and heart felt.

The Award;
Royal Visit on 6 July

The dust had hardly settled on the Jubilee weekend, before Perth was gearing up once again, this time for the Royal visit. We had been informed early in the New Year, (and well before the result of the Civic Honours competition was announced) that the Queen planned to visit Perth during her post-jubilee perambulation of the country. The details, as is usual in these circumstances, were sketchy

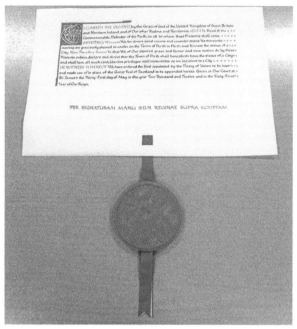

and confidential. The fact that she was coming to Perth had led to much speculation that Perth was indeed going to gain City Status, but no one could be sure.

Another parade was arranged after which the newly elected Provost presented the Queen with the ceremonial Keys of the City of Perth. These were touched by the Queen and returned to the Provost. In return the Queen presented the Provost with the Letters Patent, with the royal seal appended. At last Perth had the official document to prove that her (continuing) City Status was real and sanctioned by the monarch and not just claimed by the right of ancient usage. Following the presentation

The Letters Patent with the Royal Seal attached.
Courtesy Perth & Kinross Council

Her Majesty The Queen addressing the crowd after presenting the Letters Patent to the City of Perth.
© Angus Findlay

Her Majesty did a walk about and met many of the public.

There followed a visit to Scone Palace, where the Queen planted a memorial tree in the grounds and then there was a royal reception and official lunch in the Long Gallery of the Palace itself – a fitting Royal ceremonial finale to the City Status Campaign.

CHAPTER TWELVE

Unfinished Business – the Lord Provostship

As my term of office as Provost drew to a close, my big regret was there had not been time to reclaim for Perth the ancient title of Lord Provost. If the results of the Civic Honours competition had been announced sooner, it might have been possible. Perth's star was in the ascendant and there was good will towards it from all sides, in particular from the Scottish Government and other city councils. However, with the Council elections due six weeks after the announcement and the actual Letters Patent not to be presented to Perth for a further two months, the timing was not right.

The Lord Provostship of Perth

The concept of the Lord Provostship is deeply ingrained into all strata of society in Perth. Indeed, the sentiment is strong across the whole of Perthshire. This is remarkable because when there was a Lord Provost of Perth, his fiefdom covered only the city itself. The burghs in the county each had their own council headed by a provost. And yet, when being introduced to speak or officiate at events of all kinds and in all parts of the council area, it has been the case since 1975, when the Lord Provostship was taken away, that the provost has frequently been introduced at public meetings etc as the 'Lord Provost'.

This practice has received absolutely no official encouragement from the Council and in no Council publication has the Provost ever been referred to as the 'Lord' Provost. In spite of this it happens even when the individual making the introduction is a senior councillor or senior council officer.

Two examples will serve to illustrate how widespread the practice is, even among the most senior people. The Deputy Chief Executive of the Council (Mr Jim Irons) used the term at an important Council function (the Service Recognition Awards) in the Concert Hall in April 2011 and the First Minister, Alex Salmond, also did so in the presence of Prince Charles, Duke of Rothesay at the Charities Race Day (mentioned on p. 116). All of those who use the term 'Lord Provost' in relation to Perth know perfectly well that it is incorrect. Nevertheless they do so probably because they feel that the title brings prestige, not to the individual who happens to be the Provost, but to Perth itself, its Council and to the community of which they are a part. Undoubtedly, many of them resent the fact that it was taken away unjustly.

The Lord Provostship in Scotland

The history of the title is very similar to that of City Status. Prior to 1976, no official permission, nor any document, granting consent to use the term 'Lord Provost' was ever granted to Edinburgh, Glasgow or Perth. The use of the title, particularly with regard to Perth and Edinburgh, grew out of 'use and wont' from mediaeval times.

What happened in Dundee is worth a mention in this respect. Although prior to the sack of Dundee by Cromwell's troops in 1651, the chief magistrate was addressed as 'Lord Provost', the subsequent economic troubles and decline in Dundee's fortunes, led to the use of the title being discontinued. With the rise in prosperity due to jute, textiles and heavy engineering in the second half of the 19th Century, Dundee decided in 1887 to petition the Government for City Status and Royal authority to use the term 'Lord Provost'.

Although City Status was granted in 1889, it was a further three years (in 1892) before a Royal Warrant approving the Lord Provostship was issued. Nevertheless, following the granting of City Status, the Council assumed it would be automatic and from 1889,

styled William Hunter (Chief Magistrate 1887–1890) and Alexander Mathewson (1890–1893) as Lord Provosts of Dundee. Dundee is the only city in Scotland to have royal authority to use the title 'Lord Provost'.

Research into the history of the other important royal burghs in Scotland, in particular, Stirling, Inverness and Ayr, indicates that none of them used the title 'Lord Provost' at any time.

Lord Provostship of Perth upheld in Court

Nevertheless, the use of the term 'Lord Provost of Perth' was not unchallenged. The Government in London, unaware, no doubt of Perth's long history raised doubts about Perth's right to use the term. Eventually it came before six law lords in the High Court of Justiciary in 1836, in a case between the Lord Provost and Magistrates of Perth and His Majesty's Advocate. The question was whether to allow the designation of Lord Provost to remain and the Court decided that it should. The evidence was summarised in eight pages of text, with an Appendix of a further eight pages.[1]

The salient elements of the case were:

1. For a very long period, a use and consuetude has

_____

1 High Court of Justiciary, 10 March 1836. Minute in suspension: Magistrates of Perth against The Lord Advocate

existed, of addressing the Chief Magistrate of Perth by the title, 'Lord Provost'. He has uniformly enjoyed the title in the burgh and in correspondence on the affairs of the town. He has been called under that designation to attend the annual Convention of Burghs. He communicates with Secretaries of State and other public officials and is so addressed by them. He holds various powers and functions conferred on him under that designation by various Acts of Parliament and was introduced to the King at Holyrood House in 1822, under that title, while the Chief Magistrates of Aberdeen, Dundee, etc were presented as Provosts of their towns only. The Gazette of that time contains the address of the 'Lord Provost, Magistrates and Council of Perth', which was presented to his Majesty and acknowledged to have been received by the King.

2. Further evidence states, 'what is humbly thought to be absolutely conclusive', that the Lord Provost received the title and designation under a deed granted by the crown and bearing the signature of His Majesty George IV above the Great Seal, when appointed as a director of a Royal Institution at Perth on 5 March 1827.[2]

The universal use of the term 'Lord Provost' in legal documents and Acts of Parliament and in letters to and from Secretaries of State etc continued right up to 1975.

Different Regulations in England and Scotland

The regulations governing the Civic Honours competition in 2012 excluded the possibility of applying for the Lord Provostship and City Status simultaneously. As noted in Chapter 8 (p. 134), the civil servants and parliamentarians in London demonstrated a reprehensible ignorance of the of the situation in Scotland. They insisted that only cities which had enjoyed city status for at least 15 years could apply for a Lord Provostship. Since Inverness and Stirling were the only cities without a Lord Provost and both had been cities for less than 15 years, a Scottish competition was instituted and publicised for which there could be no eligible candidates.

Furthermore, the rules of the Civic Honours Competition (if they had been applied in Scotland)

---

2 It is ironic to note that the Royal Institution referred to was the Murray Royal Asylum, 'for the reception of lunatic persons in Perth and its neighbourhood'.

violated the legal considerations governing the restoration of a Lord Provostship, or indeed the possible granting of it *de novo*. In Scotland, the legislation is quite different from that applying in England and is different from the regulations governing City Status (which are the same in England and Scotland).

Reorganisation of Local Government

The relevant legislation is contained in *The Local Government etc (Scotland) Act 1994*, which set up the new 'all purpose' or Unitary Authorities. Section 4, Paragraphs 1 and 7 of the Act state:

> **Section 4:** Convener and Depute Convener:
>
> **Sub-section 1:** The council of each local government area shall elect a convener from among the councillors.
>
> **Sub-section 7:** The convener of each of the Councils of the cities of Aberdeen, Dundee, Edinburgh and Glasgow, shall with effect from 1 April 1996, be known by the title 'Lord Provost' and the convener of each other Council shall be known by such title as that Council may decide.
>
> Provided that no such other Council may, without the consent of the Secretary of State, decide that their convener shall be known by the title 'Lord Provost'.

The proviso is crucial. It refers to 'consent by the Secretary of State' and came about as a result of a government amendment to the Act tabled in the House of Lords. This happened because several of the Scottish peers were unhappy that the legislation, as originally drafted, would have prevented the title ever being conferred outwith the four existing cities. The Government minister at the time, Lord Peter Fraser,[3] said:

> If, therefore a Council felt that it could prove historical title to use the term 'Lord Provost', then that could be considered on its own merits. ... It would be a matter for the Secretary of State, in consultation with the Lord Lyon, if appropriate.

In the debate on this section in the Upper House, Lord Hughes quoted Perth as a possible contender for the title of 'Lord Provost'.

It is relevant to note that there is no reference in the legislation, nor in the record of the debate, of the Lord Provostship being in the gift of the crown. Indeed there is no suggestion of the monarch having any part to play in the matter. The Secretary of State's function in this respect is now devolved to the Scottish Ministers. It is not certain what the role of the Lord Lyon would be, if any.

---

3 Lord Peter Fraser was one of Perth's Advocates during the City Status campaign and attended the Westminster dinner.

The claim for a 'Lord' Provostship for Perth would appear to depend, therefore, on proving an historical title to use the term, to the satisfaction of the Scottish Ministers. I believe that the High Court case of 1836, referred to above, would be a satisfactory historical title.

What happened?

All of this was known to the new Perth & Kinross Council which was elected in May 2012. Indeed its intention to pursue the restoration of the Lord Provostship for Perth, was widely broadcast.

However, the path chosen to achieve this goal involved senior Council officers sending letters to the Civil Service in London drawing attention to the legal situation outlined above and seeking to begin moves to restore the Lord Provostship to Perth.

Initially, this drew a complete blank. There was no reply from London, not even an acknowledgement. The Civil Service did not challenge the Council's interpretation of the legal situation; they did not offer to negotiate; they remained silent.

It is known that the Government ministers and civil servants in power in Westminster in 2012 believed that the legislation that reorganised Scottish Local Government in 1975 was flawed, because it removed from the Monarch the prerogative of granting a Lord Provostship. In this respect, as in others relating to civic matters in Scotland, the civil servants and parliamentarians in London appeared to be unaware of the historical differences between Scotland and England. In fact, so far as Edinburgh Glasgow and Perth (prior to 1975) are concerned the monarch has never been involved in the award of Lord Provostships. Moreover, none of Scotland's Lord Provosts seeks to have the appointment officially ratified, or even acknowledged, by the monarch after the election.

It is said that the parliamentarians and civil servants in London believe that any future award of a Lord Provostship, should be as a result of a competition. However *The Local Government etc (Scotland) Act 1994* has already established the mechanism for granting a city the right to have a Lord Provost and the criterion to be applied (*viz* the '*ability to prove historical title*'). Furthermore, Local Government is now a devolved matter, so any change in the 1994 Act would have to be initiated and enacted by the Scottish Government.

It would appear that the civil servants who refused to respond to Perth's letters may have done so because they knew their case was weak, but believed that the Council would be unwilling to pursue the matter and provoke a confrontation.

The situation was remarkably similar to that in 2009 when the Government in London announced that there was not going to be a

City Status competition. Then Perth did not meekly accept Westminster's ruling. It responded by quoting the precedent of Cambridge in 1951 and boldly claiming City Status anyway on account of Perth's 800th anniversary. The subsequent high profile tactics which involved taking the campaign to the heart of the Government establishment in the Palace of Westminster, was supported by the Council, the public and by prominent individuals from Civic Scotland and parliamentarians from Holyrood, Westminster and Brussels. It had the desired effect and induced the Government to change its mind, paving the way for Perth's successful City Status campaign. (See p. 61).

Who knows what might have happened had a similar course of action been followed in 2012?

Lord Lieutenant

There has been concern about the position of the Lord Lieutenant of Perth & Kinross should Perth be awarded a Lord Provostship. In Edinburgh, Glasgow, Aberdeen and Dundee, the Lord Provost is *ex officio* the Lord Lieutenant.

However, this is an anomaly and although it has been the case since at least 1929, it is quite unique in the United Kingdom. Every other Lord Lieutenant in England and Scotland is appointed by the monarch. Moreover, although Perth had a Lord Provost prior to 1975, that person was not the Lord Lieutenant – the only Lord Provost who was not a Lord Lieutenant.

In fact, until 1976, what is now the council area of Perth & Kinross had two Lords Lieutenant, one for Perthshire and one for Kinross-shire. Sir David Butter was appointed Lord Lieutenant of Perthshire in 1971. Then in 1974 when the Lord Lieutenancy of Kinross-shire became vacant, Sir David was appointed to that position as well. In 1976, when the District Council of Perth & Kinross was set up, Sir David became Lord Lieutenant of Perth & Kinross. He was succeeded by Sir David Montgomery in 1995 and then by Brigadier Melville Jameson in 2006.

Regaining the title of Lord Provost would not have any bearing on the position of the current, nor any future, Lord Lieutenant of Perth & Kinross.

CHAPTER THIRTEEN

The Legacy

In 2007, when we began to plan for the Homecoming year, Perth800 and the City Status campaign, we hoped for solid achievement in terms of cultural, sporting and tourist development, an enhanced sense of identity and civic pride and a higher profile for Perth both nationally and internationally. We did not expect any direct economic benefits, apart from those that might flow from the increase in tourism etc. The official terms of the City Status competition reinforced this expectation. The Westminster Government was clear that it was a competition for Civic Honours, not for any economic benefit. There would be no pot of gold for the winner.

The broad spread of the events appealed to many different interest groups and attracted a large number of distinguished guests, including more royal visitors than had been seen in Perth for many years.

The legacy of memories was enormous and will linger in the hearts and minds of those who were involved for a very long time. But it is the economic legacy and the many cultural and sporting events that will be sustained into the future, that will matter in the long term.

In sport a number of events came to Perth for the first time. Two of them, the Tay Descent and Étape

The K2 class of kayaks at the start of the Tay Descent passing under Dunkeld Bridge. These long sleek two seater kayaks have won five of the six Tay Descents.

Caledonia, have become established annual events. In the Arts, the Concert Hall celebrated its fifth anniversary and was confirmed as one of Scotland's major arts and conference venues. Meanwhile, Perth Theatre is undergoing a major refurbishment. When it re-opens in 2017, with its Edwardian auditorium refurbished, a new 200 seat studio theatre and its other facilities modernised, a new chapter in Perth's illustrious contribution to Scotland's theatre scene will begin.

On the wider front Perth has developed its reputation as a vibrant small European city, capable of

Paul Cummins' The Weeping Window installation at Balhousie Castle.

installation was enormous. For many it can be likened to a pilgrimage in remembrance of the First World War, with bus loads of Veterans {and others}, from all over Scotland and thousands of individuals and families making their way to Perth.

More important than all of this, however, was Perth's standing amongst the communities of Scotland. Now, with city status acknowledged officially, Perth could once again play an important role in the economic and cultural development of Scotland.

Perth was immediately accepted as an equal by the other cities of Scotland and our success was applauded across Scotland, Europe and North America, especially by our twin cities and widespread diaspora.

Seventh City?

Nevertheless to refer to Perth as the seventh city of Scotland (as many do) is to acquiesce with the fiction, which we had spent so much time and effort contradicting, that Perth was not a city prior to 2012. As we have seen, Perth could claim to be one of the first cities of Scotland and its title as the official Second City was upheld in 1602 by the highest courts of the land. (See Chapter 2). Thereafter until 1975 it was consistently and correctly, referred to as the *City and*

hosting major cultural and sporting events, which will attract large numbers of visitors from home and overseas.

An outstanding example was Paul Cummins' *Weeping Window* Installation set up at the refurbished Balhousie Castle (as yet the only location in mainland Scotland[1] where it has been seen). The response to the

---

1   The Government has not yet announced the programme for the latter half of the 14–18 – NOW centenary tour. So far the only locations in Scotland have been the St Magnus Cathedral in Kirkwall, Orkney and Balhousie Castle in Perth.

Royal Burgh of Perth. Certainly in Perth, if not generally in Scotland, it is reckoned that Perth's ancient City Status has been *restored*, rather than granted *de novo*.

The Economic legacy

Although the rules of the competition emphasised that the Government in London would not provide any economic benefits for successful cities, Edinburgh was not listening. Very soon after the departure of HM the Queen, Perth & Kinross Council was informed of an unexpected, but very welcome, financial consequence of City Status.

The City Heritage Trust Funds

In February 2012 Historic Scotland had offered grants of £7.69m to the City Heritage Trusts of Scotland's existing cities. This was to help facilitate the regeneration of the built environment of Scotland's cities and make them more attractive for people to live in and more welcoming for potential investors. Perth, of course, was not included.

However, in July 2012, just days after the Queen had presented the Letters Patent to the Provost, the Scottish Government offered the new city £650,000 to set up the Perth City Heritage Fund, which was in fact Perth's share of Historic Scotland's funding for the City Heritage Trusts, announced earlier. In Perth's case, the fund was to be administered by the Perth and Kinross Heritage Trust, a registered Scottish Charity which since 1988 has sought to conserve

and promote archaeology and architectural heritage for the benefit of residents, visitors and future generations.

The Perth City Heritage Fund was to be used between 2012 and 2015 to safeguard and enhance the historic environment of Perth, by part funding, with the private sector, the repair and upgrading of buildings in the Conservation Areas of the city

It was an early pointer to the fact that City Status was going to be about much more than dignity and Civic Honours and would have major financial consequences that would have by-passed Perth if the Civic Honours Competition had not been held, or if Perth had not been successful. In its three years of operation the fund has facilitated over 30 projects in Perth, ranging in gross value from a few hundred pounds to over £200,000.

Perhaps the most obvious has been the refurbishment of the almost derelict building above the King's Arms or Cunningham Graham Close, at No 15 High Street – the oldest

The Logo of the Perth & Kinross Heritage Trust.

The logo of the Perth City Heritage Fund.

King's Arms, or Cunningham Graham Close. Newly refurbished with lime harl. The oldest inhabited building in Perth dating from the late 1600s.

The corner of George Street and the High Street. In the centre is 1–3 George Street, stone faced with red windows, dating from 1780. Kings Arms Close is the yellow coloured building to the right.

John Buchan's Birthplace (20 York Place) is the right hand side of this semi-detached Victorian villa.

The most recent project involved upgrading the neighbouring building, Nos 1–3 George Street. This four story Georgian tenement built in about 1780, has also been refurbished inside and out, with new sash and casement windows painted the original red colour. The stonework, in this case, has been left bare as it was originally and not painted or covered with a lime render.

Refurbishing these old buildings not only improves the environment and adds interest to the street, but, by upgrading the flats inside, many of which were derelict and empty, provides good quality homes for rent and helps to repopulate and revive the city centre.

In 2015 a second tranche of Government money was allocated to the City Heritage Trusts of Scotland's seven cities. On this occasion Perth's share was £750,000. Among the projects that this money has supported is the restoration of No 20 York Place, the C-listed birthplace of John Buchan, (Later Lord Tweedsmuir) the author of *The 39 Steps*. The building had been empty and neglected for some time, but the outside has been refurbished and the interior converted to offices. It is now occupied by the charity, Mindspace.

The Six Cities Alliance

After the Holyrood elections in 2007, which resulted in a minority SNP Government, Scottish politicians had become increasingly aware of the importance of cities in driving the economy of the whole country forward. And so policies to promote

inhabited building in Perth, dating from the late 1600s. The crumbling harl on the outside of the building has been chipped away and replaced with a lime render and painted a traditional yellow ochre colour. The common stairway has been refurbished, the windows replaced and the flats inside brought up to a modern standard.

the competitiveness of Scottish cities in relation to those in England and overseas, were actively promoted. The Government's commitment to this concept was emphasised by the appointment of Nicola Sturgeon MSP, then the Deputy First Minister, to be the 'Minister for Cities'. This process emphasised the crucial importance of achieving success in the City Status campaign. The baleful consequences of failure were just as obvious.

Following the next Scottish Parliamentary elections in May 2011, at which the SNP was re-elected with an overall majority, the attitude towards cities became even more pro-active. One of the Government's earliest actions, on 19 May, just two weeks after the election, was to launch the *Six Cities Alliance* in Stirling. Attending the inauguration were senior councillors and officers from Edinburgh, Glasgow, Aberdeen, Dundee, Inverness and Stirling, along with officials from the Scottish Government and the Scottish Council Development & Industry (SCDI).

Perth, of course, was not invited. Indeed at that time our application for City Status was still in the final stage of preparation and had not yet been submitted. However, rather surprisingly, representatives from Perth were invited to all the subsequent meetings of the *Alliance*. Along with the Deputy Leader of the Council and senior officers from the Economic Development Department, I attended a meeting in June 2011 in Edinburgh to follow up the launch of the *Six Cities Alliance* the previous month. We were then invited to a 'Policy Challenge' Dinner in Stirling to develop the strategy and later a conference in Glasgow in December. The situation of the Perth delegation at these events was very ambiguous. Some of the other attendees referred to the group as the 'Six Cities Plus One Alliance', which indicated a well of good will for Perth. Nevertheless we were acutely aware of the provisional nature of our membership.

At the conference in December, Ms Sturgeon launched the '*Agenda for Cities*', the subtitle of which was, '*Delivering for Scotland. In collaboration with Aberdeen, Dundee, Edinburgh, Glasgow, Inverness and Stirling.* The 'Agenda' was to be facilitated on behalf of the Scottish Government by the SCDI. Dr Lesley Sawers,[2] its Chief Executive said, '*Scottish cities are the economic, cultural, social and intellectual powerhouses of Scotland, They are distinct and different, but their success is essential to Scotland's longterm future. The success of our cities is vital to the regions and rural communities that surround them. The Six Cities agenda is an opportunity for all of Scotland's cities*

---

2 Dr Sawers was one of Perth's Advocates. She wrote the following comment, which was included in the Claim Document: Scotland's cities are a major source of national pride and a driver for many parts of the Scotland's economy. We believe the economic impact generated by the creation of the City of Perth would benefit all of Scotland, particularly the distinct geographical area to become the Perth City region.

to work with each other, the Scottish Government and other organisations to deliver our shared ambitions for economic success'.

The Scottish Cities Alliance took a little while to establish itself and develop a provisional programme focusing on infrastructure, low carbon and *Smart Cities* initiatives. An early success was achieved when European funding was secured to develop the strategy and by 2014 an ambitious set of City Investment plans totalling £10bn had been developed by the Government, SCDI and the seven Local Authorities involved.

Perth has been the first of Scotland's cities to progress from the drawing board of the Scottish Cities Alliance to an agreement with a company to invest in a major new development. This will be a £30m project of houses, shops and other facilities, including a multi-storey car park at Thimblerow. This will build a new community and breathe new life into the western part of the city.

The prize for success in the City Status campaign has been to be part of these exciting new developments in Scottish politics. Perth will contribute to and benefit from the new energy which is flowing from the Scottish Government through the Cities Alliance to the individual city authorities.

Prior Knowledge?

I reflected later on these matters and wondered whether some senior government officials were privy to the fact that Perth would be successful and had prepared the way for its role as a city. In particular I speculated on:

- the unconstitutional inclusion of Perth in the early meetings of the Six Cities Alliance;

- the notification, long before the winners of the Civic Honours Competition were announced, that the Queen would visit Perth during her post-jubilee tour;

- and the allocation of £650,000 from the Heritage Fund so soon after Perth's success.

Even one of these would have been unusual, two would be a remarkable co-incidence, but three…?

CHAPTER FOURTEEN

Beyond City Status

Back to Reality

Perth's fortunes reached a peak in July of 2012. The award of City Status in March had induced a sense of euphoria which lasted right through the summer. With the exception of the City Heritage Fund, however, all of the new developments, however exciting, would take time to come to fruition. Meanwhile, Perth settled in to its new status as an official city of Scotland. There was not much evidence outwardly of the change, because in fact Perth had always referred to itself as a City. However, the gateway signs on entering Perth were changed, emphasising the City's new credentials.

After the summer recess, reality began to bite back. The budgetary pressures on councils across Scotland had been building for several years. Prudent management of Perth's finances (singled out for praise by Audit Scotland) ensured that Perth & Kinross was among the most sure-footed of councils in balancing the diminishing supply of finance with the increasing demand for services. Nevertheless, there had been cuts to budgets, including to those that affected the City Status campaign. An early casualty, for example, was the group of officers from Education Services who had promoted the Global Conference in 2009 and worked on the twinning strategy and

the Europe Prize (See p. 44). This curtailed our ability to develop new international initiatives and even to continue with established events.

Moreover, there had also been several unwelcome developments affecting Perth in the last 30 years, the cumulative effect of which has had a debilitating effect on the city's morale, even if their effect on Perth's economic statistics were surprisingly small. One by one the iconic businesses upon which Perth built its reputation for innovation and entrepreneurship have been closed down or emasculated.

Whisky

Although whisky has continued to be a booming industry all over Scotland, the direct contribution of the huge whisky businesses which were once headquartered in Perth has gradually dwindled and will reach zero with the impending closure of Edrington's Famous Grouse marketing division at Kinfauns.

One of the Gateway signs at the entrance to Perth.

The European marketing division of Edrington Distillers at Kinfauns, overlooking the Tay.

Profile bust of Sir Stanley Norie-Miller BT, MC, DL, JP, on a retaining wall in the Norie-Miller Garden. On his death in 1993, Sir Stanley bequeathed the park to the City of Perth.

There are, of course, several malt distilleries in Perthshire, including Glenturret, near Crieff which is the oldest and is the home of the Famous Grouse Experience. Another is Edradour in Pitlochry which was, until the recent commissioning of several new distilleries, the smallest. Only Genturret, of the established distilleries in Perthshire, is now Scottish owned.

Insurance

General Accident was once a world player in the insurance industry and the Norie-Miller father and son, who ran the company for 80 years, were men of great substance in Perth and indeed in Scotland.

Now, of course, the crucial family connection between the city and the management of the company has been severed and while General Accident's erstwhile head office at Pitheavlis is still a 'centre of excellence' in the AVIVA empire (see below), the whole enterprise is vulnerable to the stroke of the pen of a Chief Executive with no particular connection to Perth.

Retail

For many years, Perth has taken great pride in its independent retailers who cater for niche markets and provide an unrivalled breadth of shopping experience for locals and tourists. Although in recent years, the retail sector has been hard hit in Perth as elsewhere with shops closing and footfall declining, there is a host of small independent retailers in the heart of the city, still holding their

Top right

An Edwardian terrace of small shops, with flats above, in Methven Street.

Below right

McEwens independent department store, now closed.

own among the hairdressers, coffee shops and take-away bars. Nevertheless, when McEwen's, the last independent department store in Scotland and the standard bearer of Perth's retail sector succumbed, it sent a shock wave through the city.

The Mart

But perhaps the most serious loss was the closure of the Perth Mart and the transfer of its auction sales, especially the famous Perth Bull sales, to a new mart near Stirling. This was a blow to Perth on many levels. It was not just the bull sales that mattered, but also the less newsworthy sales of sheep, store cattle, ponies and stallions. The shops, restaurants and hotels all suffered and so also did the professional and commercial services which support the agricultural community – banks, accountants, lawyers, motor traders etc.

Much more important, however, is the loss of the prestige that came from the centrality of Perth within its county as swathes of the rural community no longer look to Perth for their regular contact with the agricultural community. And of course, Perth's loss is Stirling's gain.

While the star of whisky's importance to Perth burned brightly for 150 years or so and insurance for much less than that, Perth's prosperity since the Middle Ages has been built on agriculture and especially on livestock. Moreover, its mart was the most important in central Scotland for generations. Its loss is a grievous blow.

The Harbour

Still trading, but with its viability seriously questioned, is Perth's harbour. Along with its quays and tender (*The Fair Maid*), the harbour is owned by the Perth Common Good Fund although the Council has assumed financial responsibility for it. It was the key to Perth's mediaeval prosperity and central to its claim to be Scotland's first capital.

The original harbour and main

commercial port, was at the foot of the High Street. It was complimented by Greyfriars Harbour, where the southern arm of the Lade opened into the river. (See picture p. 18) Here ship-building and other related activities took place. During the second half of the 19th century

The last of the Perth Bull sales. Courtesy of the *Perthshire Advertiser*

Below left
Perth Harbour showing its extensive quays. Sadly, it is empty as is too often the case.

Below right
The harbour tender, The Fair Maid.

both these harbours were in decline and ships berthed at various quays along what is now Shore Road (*Coal Quay* and *Lime Quay*) and at *Friarton*, where the present harbour was built.

Unlike the mart, the harbour has not been an important part of Perth's economy for several decades, but it is, nevertheless, a vital link to Perth's illustrious past. Moreover, with the railway line adjacent and the motorway close by, it has the potential to be a rail, sea and road interchange. On these grounds alone it is worth making strenuous efforts to revive it.

Other industries

And there are other industries that have peaked and fallen away: in particular the salmon fisheries, the high profile decorative glass industry and even Pullars of Perth a hundred years ago. Not only did these businesses contribute significantly to Perth's economy, they also reinforced its identity and reputation. They ensured that the name of 'Perth' was recognised across the UK.

Perth's Economy in Numbers

And yet, in spite of all this, Perth is still a prosperous and growing community. Over the last 20 years its population has been one of the most buoyant of any local authority in Scotland. Unemployment across Perth & Kinross hovers at around half the Scottish average and a high proportion of adults of working age are employed. Furthermore, in the

City centre the proportion of vacant shops (8.2 per cent at the time of writing) has been consistently among the lowest in Scotland and the business start-up rate one of the highest.

A New Future for Perth

If Perth is not just to prosper, but to stand out as a city in the 21st century, the black holes in it's commercial and industrial firmament, need to be replaced by new stars that will shine brightly for Perth – and not just in economic terms. Perth needs men and women who will demonstrate that the city is still a home for entrepreneurs and innovators who are committed to Perth and Perthshire as well as to their businesses.

And indeed there are some shining stars among the businesses of Perth.

Stagecoach

Perhaps the international company most closely identified with Perth is the bus company Stagecoach – set up by Sir Brian Souter and his sister Anne Gloag. The Souter family, including the older brother, David, who became a Church of Scotland minister in Perth, is quite remarkable. Brought up in a tenement flat in Perth, they built up the company to

The familiar red orange and blue livery of a Stagecoach bus.

become the global organisation that it now is, running bus and rail services in the UK and across the world from the USA to China. Meanwhile the international headquarters remains in premises on the Dunkeld Road in Perth and the family retains its Perth focus and its common touch. They all live locally and maintain close links with the religious life of the city.

Not since AK Bell has Perth had local entrepreneurs with the wealth and philanthropic potential of Sir Brian Souter and Anne Gloag.

Other Global companies

Perth hosts the headquarters of a number of other global companies, which bring a large number of very well paid staff to Perth and also support a range of business services from banks to architects and sponsor arts and sporting organisations. None of them, however, is identified with Perth in the way that Stagecoach is.

Scottish & Southern Energy (SSE)

The jewel in Perth's business crown is Scottish & Southern Energy, which occupies a huge site adjacent to the Inveralmond Roundabout. It was set up in 1943 by the war time Secretary of State for Scotland, Tom Johnston, as the North of Scotland Hydro Electricity Board and its purpose was to design, construct and manage hydro-electricity projects in the Highlands.

After privatisation and with its HQ moved from Edinburgh to Perth, it merged with Southern Electricity to become Scottish and Southern

Left
The Headquarters of SSE on the Dunkeld Road.

Top right
The instantly recognisable label of Highland Spring bottled water. Very much a Scottish, but not obviously a Perthshire product.

Energy (SSE) and is now the largest company registered in Scotland. As a major player in the renewables industry it is involved in an industrial sector that is very important in Perthshire and in Scotland as a whole and it receives a great deal of attention from the Scottish Government.

Nevertheless, perhaps because of its very size and diversity It is seen generally as one of the 'Big Six' UK energy companies and not as an essentially Scottish, far less a Perth, firm.

Highland Spring

Based in Blackford some 16 miles west of Perth, Highland Spring is the biggest producer of naturally sourced bottled water in the UK. Although foreign owned, It is an innovative and expanding company, with a very

well known brand. However, it is generally seen as Scottish company, not particularly identified with Perth.

AVIVA

Perth lost its headquarters function in insurance when the General Accident merged with the Commercial Union in 1998, to become CGU. Then CGU joined Norwich Union to become the CGNU, with headquarters in London and shortly afterwards changed its name to AVIVA – an invented name symbolising 'life'. The company operates in 16 countries around the world and has 31 million customers, 13 million of them in the UK.

AVIVA occupies the General Accident's Pitheavlis offices – an innovative concrete structure built into the side of Craigie Hill, affording panoramic views over Perth to the north and east. It employs over 1,000 people in Perth, which is one of seven 'Centres of Excellence' in the company. The main function of the Perth centre is to manage household claims. It is also host to the staff pensions team and the specialist legal team.

Vector Aerospace

This is a global aero-engineering company, which is based in Canada,

but has a major factory in Almondbank on the outskirts of Perth. It provides maintenance, repair and overhaul (MRO) services for all kinds of military and civil aircraft and helicopters.

SMEs Perth's Industrial base

Notwithstanding these very large companies, the bedrock of Perth's prosperity and the reason for its buoyant employment statistics, lies in its innovative small and medium sized enterprises (SMEs), some of which have a global reach and most of which are locally owned and managed. It is very important for the future of Perth that as these firms develop, that they identify with their home city and in turn that Perth itself recognises and reflects the prestige of a successful company. It would be impossible to mention all the enterprising SMEs in Perth, but a few deserve special attention.

Morrison and Mackay

A whisky business which is still family owned and locally managed is Morrison and MacKay,[1] based in Bankfoot some eight miles north of Perth. The family has a long pedigree in the whisky business and is actively involved in developing whisky liqueurs. More importantly for the long term, they have resuscitated and are actively marketing the *Old Perth* brand of blended malt whisky. In order to satisfy the basic

---

1 Formerly the Scottish Liqueur Centre.

requirements for this brand and for their liqueurs, they are building a new malt distillery near Abernethy.

Merlin ERD

Perhaps the most significant rising star in Perth's industrial firmament is Merlin ERD (Extended Reach Drilling). Still a small company, but with global ambitions, Merlin ERD now operates in over 30 countries across the world. It provides innovative technologies and expert drilling and engineering services to the international oil and gas sector.

The objective is to reduce costs and extend wells further and deeper to release reserves trapped in difficult locations. In 2016 Merlin ERD won the Queen's Award for Excellence in International Trade for the second time. (The first was in 2014).

Iain Hutchison, the owner and managing director of the company is an aviation enthusiast. It was he who piloted the spitfire which wowed the crowd during the parade on 'Perth Day' the 2nd July 2010 (See p. 88). And the name of his company 'Merlin' comes from the Rolls Royce engine which powered the spitfire and hurricane fighters and the Lancaster bombers during World War II.

Spectraglass

Based on the Inveralmond industrial estate, where it has just invested £1m in a new factory, Spectraglass continues Perth's illustrious tradition

The prestigious HQ building of Merlin ERD in Cherrybank Gardens, Perth.

Inspired marketing. Merlin ERD sponsor the Spitfire at Edinburgh airport.

of innovative glass manufacture. Its main line of business for many years has been manufacturing pressure gauges for steam boilers that are used in the oil and gas industry. In recent times they have moved into decorative architectural work, in particular making stylish kitchen worktops and glass hearths for wood burning stoves.

Their most unusual contract has been to produce the special glass cylinders for modified Davy lamps. Four of these have been used at each Olympic Games (summer and winter), since Lake Placid in 1980, including the most recent event in Rio. Because of the strict regulations about naked flames in aircraft the lamps are required to keep the olympic flame alight whenever it travels by air.

Binn Group

Established at Glenfarg over 20 years ago by father and son John and Allan MacGregor as a landfill site and farm diversification project, the Binn Group has become Scotland's leading provider of integrated recycling and waste management Services.

It has recently moved into renewable energy involving landfill gas, wind power and micro-hydro and is embarking on Scotland's first eco-innovation park which will use waste energy to heat poly tunnels in which to grow fruit and vegetables.

An Aviation Hub at Scone

A number of enterprising organisations, – business, academic, commercial and recreational – are now located at Perth Airport, about two miles north of the Perth boundary.

Morris Leslie Group

The Group own the airfield, having purchased it in 1996. Morris Leslie established the company over 40 years ago as a plant hire and commercial auction business on the disused airfield at Errol, just east of Perth. It has expanded considerably since then into modular buildings and plant hire and has a significant plant hire business in England. Although Morris Leslie is not involved in aviation himself, he has a keen interest in developing the airfield.

ACS Aviation

ACS Aviation is the licensed operator of the airfield and provides all types pilot training up to multi-engine commercial pilot's licenses. Its engineering department operates out of the largest general aviation hangar in Scotland and provides maintenance services for all types of fixed wing aircraft and helicopters, for commercial and private operators.

Modified miners' Davy lamp used to keep the Olympic flame alight while in transit by air.

The Scottish Charities Air Ambulance taking off from Scone Airport.
Courtesy SCAA.

Scottish Charity Air Ambulance

The SCAA was set up in Scone in May 2013. It operates alongside state funded air-sea rescue aircraft and is controlled from the Scottish Ambulance Service base at Cardonald and carries Scottish Ambulance Service paramedics. In its first year it flew nearly 300 missions. Since October 2015 the aircraft used has been a Eurocopter EC-135.

Scottish Aero Club

This is the oldest flying club in Scotland, having been formed in 1956 by the amalgamation of the Scottish Flying Club (founded in 1927) and the Strathtay Aero Club (founded in 1936). The membership is strong with over 200 pilot members and many aircraft based at Scone.

AST and Perth College (UHI)

Air Services Training is a relatively small, but long lived company, with roots extending back in England to 1931 and in Scone to 1936. It provides training for aeronautical engineers and is the oldest such establishment in the world.

It is now a wholly owned subsidiary of Perth College UHI. Its main activity is to deliver training courses for professional aeronautical engineers so that they can meet the various European Aviation Safety Agency (EASA) standards. Also as part of the University of the Highlands and Islands it runs academic courses for the B.Eng.(hons) degree. An important additional activity is to provide consultancy services to the aviation industry.

The academic classes take place in the Brahan building of Perth College, while the practical skills are taught in the large hangar at Perth airport. It is the preferred training provider for several national and international airlines, including British Airways, Cathay Pacific, British Midland, Easy Jet and Bristol Helicopters. It also trains military aeronautical engineers for the British Army Air corps and the Air Forces of Kuwait and Oman.

It is a company that punches well above its weight in international business, having established satellite training establishments in Iceland, Jordan, Kuwait and Indonesia and with India and Pakistan awaiting approval. In 2015 AST won the Queen's Award for Excellence in International Trade.

The Agricultural Sector

Notwithstanding the loss of the Mart, Perth is still the centre of a huge agricultural county, which comes together most publicly at the Perth Show – perhaps the most significant of all Perth's annual events

Top
The Jetstream aircraft in the hangar in Scone. It is used to train students in avionics.
Courtesy AST.

The AST logo. When AST moved from Hamble in England to merge with Airwork in Perth in 1960, it changed its logo. Originally the globe was surmounted by a sphinx. This was changed to the double headed eagle to emphasise the company's new location in and commitment to Perth.
Courtesy AST

The grand Livestock parade at the Perth Show.

which focus on particular products. Among these are *Mackie's Crisps*, which are manufactured in a new factory near Errol, *Simon Howie*, which is now a very large butchery business, *Summer Harvest*, which exports its rapeseed oil even to Dubai, *Scarlett's of Meigle* and *Heather Hills Honey Farm* which supply the inexhaustible demand for Scottish heather honey.

Restaurants, cafés, hotels and visitor attractions

– and also at the Farmers Markets. Food and drink are Scotland's most important exports and Perthshire's agricultural businesses feature prominently in many sectors, in particular beef and lamb, soft fruit, potatoes, turnips and of course, whisky.

As well as livestock mostly on the upland areas, soft fruit (now almost exclusively in poly tunnels), potatoes in the east of the county and a large arable sector, there is a long list of specialist agricultural businesses,

While farming, manufacturing and commercial companies are vital for the stability of Perth's economy, the tourist and hospitality businesses are cumulatively Perth's biggest employers.

There is a wide range of hotels guesthouses and bed and breakfast establishments within the city and a new five star hotel is about to be built on the eastern edge of the city, at Kinfauns. Just outside Perth are several excellent country house hotels and not far away are Gleneagles and Crieff Hydro.

The most visible business

Andrew Scarlett, chairman of the Perthshire Farmers' Market, and his daughter, discuss the production of heather honey with Prince Charles.
© Angus Findlay

Salutation Hotel. The oldest hotel in Scotland, and certainly operational in the late 1600s. The façade has recently been restored, and the magnificent Venetian window and statues of Black Watch soldiers are pristine.

expansion in Perth in recent years has been in the number of cafés and restaurants. If Perth's reputation for the variety of its shops has been eclipsed by the internet, it has been replaced by a growing appreciation of the diversity of its eating establishments. These vary from branches of the multinational coffee shop chains, to locally owned gourmet restaurants of the highest calibre. Many serve the very best of Scottish ingredients and in others you can sample a variety of menus originating from Europe, Asia and South America.

Perth's visitor attractions are developing steadily. Two of the most important, Scone Palace and Balhousie Castle Museum, have recently moved up market from four to five stars in VisitScotland's

Left
Perth's continental café culture is alive and well on a warm summer afternoon.

Above
Dean's, on the corner of Atholl Street and Kinnoull Street, one of the best of Perth's gourmet restaurants.

Below
Scone Palace, from the south.

Fergusson gallery devoted to the Scottish Colourist, J. D. Fergusson, and his wife the dancer Margaret Morris.

Below

Willowgate ponds offer safe angling for rainbow trout, with the possibility of a cup of coffee and a scone afterwards in the café in the restored bothy.

Bottom

The base for the Perth Sailing club, in the shadow of the Friarton Bridge.

classification. Perth's Concert Hall, the Museum & Art Gallery, the Fergusson Gallery, St John's Kirk and St Ninian's cathedral, all contribute to the mix of visitor attractions.

Exploiting the Tay

Although the River Tay was the *raison d'être* for Perth's very existence and provides a stunning foreground for pictures of the city, it has not been exploited to Perth's advantage since demise of the salmon netting industry. That has begun to change.

At Willowgate, beneath the Friarton Bridge, Mr David Clark and the Tay and Earn Trust have created lagoons alongside the river which are stocked with rainbow trout. Here young anglers can learn the sport and older ones can enjoy some relaxed fishing in peaceful safe circumstances. Alongside is a fishing bothy which has been tastefully restored and is now a café and shop.

Down-river a few hundred yards is the base for the Perth Sailing Club and a little further down, the Tay and Earn Trust is developing a water sports centre to cater especially for canoeing and rowing.

Even more exciting are the plans to develop water taxis and river cruises. Three floating pontoons which will be lifted out of the water during the winter, have been commissioned. They will be installed at a base on Tay Street opposite the Fergusson Gallery, at Willowgate and at Elcho Castle, about two miles downriver from the Friarton Bridge. Eventually it may be feasible to provide cruises down to Newburgh and the new V&A Museum at Dundee.

What next for Perth?

Achieving City Status has been a catalyst for positive change in Perth. Without it, Perth & Kinross would have become part of the Dundee City Region and would inevitably have been under the influence of a Dundee-centric administration. This was Perth's experience during the years of the Tayside Region (1975–1996) and no one in Perth & Kinross wants to repeat it.

Thankfully the centrality of Perth within its own city region was secured. Furthermore, as exciting policies are developed to take advantage of the multi-million pound Tayside and Fife City Deal, Perth's status as a city, equal with Dundee, will ensure a twin city approach. This will be enormously important in maintaining Perth's separate identity into the future.

For Perth to prosper as a small but vibrant European city it must try to position its appeal skilfully. Scotland's four big cities are in a separate league. Inverness over 100 miles to the north and capital of the huge Highland region, has a niche of its own. Perth's main competitor is Stirling. Its strategy should be to develop the agricultural, industrial and commercial sectors which underpin its economy. At the same time it should build up its links with the Perth campus of the University of the Highlands and Islands. Then it should seek to exploit its location at the hub of Scotland and gateway to the Highlands.

With these foundations consolidated, Perth can turn its

Exploring the potential of tourism on the River Tay. With me, from right to left, John Swinney, local MSP and Deputy First Minister, David Clark, Chairman of the Tay and Earn Trust, Jim Findlay, head development, and Iain Valentine.

attention to its tourist industry which has a huge potential to lift its economy and also to provide a better quality of life for its citizens. The objective must be to secure Perth's status as a distinctive and important city in Scotland.

The most obvious way into the future is to invest in the cultural, sporting and landscape potential of the whole of Perth and Kinross and harness the entrepreneurial and innovative skills of its people to develop a 21st century tourist industry. It is not possible to separate the city from its hinterland. The modern tourist may well visit the Queen's View above Loch Tummel in the morning, play a round of golf at Gleneagles in the afternoon and enjoy a gourmet meal in a restaurant in Perth in the evening. And for younger, more active people there are many possibilities – climbing and hill walking, extreme sports on the river or in the mountains and perhaps a visit to one of the bars or night clubs in the evening.

As this book goes to press, Perth is girding its loins to mount a forceful challenge to become UK City of Culture in 2021. The competition will be stiff, but no more so than it was for City Status. While success is not assured, the omens are good and if it comes to pass it will bring enormous investment and enable Perth to develop its city credentials.

Conclusion

Perth's prosperity in the past has been based on its position at the geopolitical centre of Scotland, at an important crossing of the Tay and at the gap in the Highland Fault line. Its future as a city of Scotland will depend on similar factors, but especially on its hub position in Scotland's transport network.

By cooperating with the Scottish Cities Alliance and contributing forcefully in the negotiations around the Tayside and Fife City Deal, Perth can develop a dynamic industrial and commercial foundation. With the centre secure, Perth could then become the hub for a mobile tourist industry embracing all the best of landscape, culture and sport. Perth could then reach out to Loch Leven and Kinross in the south, Crieff and Auchterarder in the west, Aberfeldy, Pitlochry and the A9 corridor to the north and Blairgowrie and the Tay estuary in the east.

At the very centre of this web lies the City of Perth, with its people, its business, arts and civic organisations and its Local Authority. Perth has enormous potential.

Index

3SCOTS 50, 51, 81, 86, 90, 91, 150
4SCOTS 154
7SCOTS 50, 52, 54, 81, 86, 91
51st Highland 50, 54–57
ACS Aviation 178
AST 179
Aberdeen 9, 11, 23, 25, 26, 29, 33, 37, 152
Aberdeen *Press and Journal* 69
Aberfeldy 81, 91
Abernethy 15, 19, 74, 93
Advocates for Perth 59, 60, 142, 169
After Silence 114
Allan, David (artist) 75
Andermas Mediaeval Fair 107
Anderson, Dr. Adam 95
Angles 15, 20, 28
Antonine Guard 106
Arkwright, Richard 78
Armagh 28–31, 149
Ars Antiqua Choir 118
Art and Design Exhibition 101
Aschaffenburg 45, 84, 113, 121, 122, 153
Auchterarder 13
Audit Commission 67, 68
Auld, Edna 97, 152
Auld Alliance 22
Australian String Quartet 114
AVIVA 172, 176
Ayr 33, 139
Aytoun Hall 13

Balhousie Castle & Museum 51, 81, 126, 166, 182
Baltic sea 20
Banks, Gordon MP 68, 69, 140
Battle of Britain 58
Battle of Largs 22
Battle of the Clans 101, 102
Bean, Roland 96
Beating Retreat 91, 92
Bell's Sports centre 41
Berger, Mr Eric 56, 57
Bernicia 15
Bertha Park 138
Berwick-upon-Tweed 9, 20–23
Bidwells 145
Big Sing 101
Binn Group 178

Black Watch 50–52, 81, 143
Black Watch Regiment 88
Black Watch Association 81
Blackadder, Dame Elizabeth 104
Blackfriars Monastery 14, 22–24
Blacksmith (painting) 46
Blair Atholl Water Mill 80
Blue Grass Festival 120
Bloom competitions 42
Brady, Luke 100
Brechin 29
Bridge (mediaeval) 19
Brisbane, Mr Gair 58
Britons 15
Broxden 97, 98
Brown, Gordon MP 70
Buildings of Scotland 76
Burghs 20, 21
Burma Campaign 57, 58
Burma Star Association 57
Burns, Robert 38, 75
Buttercup, The, (Jig) 100
Bydgoszcz 47, 84, 119, 122, 154

Cadets 88
Café culture 42, 10h
Cairn O' Mohr 80
Cambridge 30, 62, 63, 164
Camel race 116
Cameron, David MP 141
Canterbury 133
Capital City 14
Cardiff 29
Cairncross 126
Carpow Log Boat 93
Carse, Alexander (Artist) 75
Carthusian Monastery 23, 24, 35
Cartwright, Lt. Col. Stephen 51
Cassells, Dr Ian 80
Catholic Church 24
Catmoor Burn 17
Charities Race Day 116
Chan, John 91
Chelsea, Viscount 69
Cheltenham 149
Chess Festival 110
Chillingworth, Bishop David 85
Christie, Rt. Rev. John 85

Christmas lights 96
Church Council 12
Church of Scotland 3
Cittaslow 42–44 104
City Hall 105
City Heritage Trust Fund 167, 171
City of Culture 184
City of Perth Sinfonia 119
City wall 19
Clark, David 183
Coats of Arms 26, 27
Cognac 45, 84, 153
Concert Hall 37, 41, 52, 74, 90, 92, 98, 105, 114, 159, 165, 182
Convention of Burghs 24, 25
Council of Twelve 22
Council Chambers 65
Courier 69, 143, 148, 149
Court of Session 25
Craig, Dr Carol 44,
Craigclowan school 118
Cruachan 51
Cunningham Graham Close 167
Curling 110–112

Dal Riata 15, 16, 19
Davy Lamp 178
Diamond Jubilee 9, 11
Dean of Guild 14
Derby 30
Double headed eagle 26, 27
Dover House 68
Duke of Edinburgh Award 86
Dumfries 33, 139
Dunadd 16, 19
Dunblane 36
Duncan, Prof. AAM 22, 137
Dundee 9, 11, 14, 24–26, 29, 37, 152, 160
Dundurn 16
Dunfermline 21, 34, 139
Dunkeld 36, 108

Early Day Motion 68
Edinburgh 9, 11, 12, 14, 18– 21, 23–27, 29, 32, 33, 37, 160
Edrington distillers 97, 171
Edward, Sir David 123, 146, 152
Edwards, Ina 104
Elgin 138
Elizabeth Cross 82, 88
Elsasser, Bürgermeister Werner 85, 90
Étape Caledonia 110, 165
Europe Prize 42, 44,

Europa Nostra Award 79
European diploma 45
European Flag of Honour 44, 45
Executioner 107
Exley, Ms Mandy 69

Façade scheme 127
'Fair' City 9, 12, 42
Fair Maid of Perth 9, 10, 33, 42, 48, 151
Fair Maid's House 66, 129
Fairlie, Andrew 80
Fairlie, Jim 80
Fallon, Sir Michael MP 68, 69, 140, 146
Famous Grouse mascot 156
Famous Grouse statue 97
Farmers' Market 43, 79, 80, 180
Fenik, John 155
Fenton, Lt. Col 86, 150
Fergusson Gallery 41, 182, 183
Filharmonia Pomorska 119
Fireworks 105, 106, 136
Fleet, Chris 94
Flodden 23
Forteviot 9, 15, 19, 74, 93
Fortriu 15
Fraser, Lord Peter 69, 162
Fraser, Murdo 140
Freedom of Perth 52, 53, 54
Freshwater Fisheries Research Station 130
Fyffe, John 44

G8 summit 13, 38
Gaelic 17
Game Fair 90, 91
Gaul, Linda 99
Gdansk 47
Gannochy Trust 125
Gebertt, Dr Stanislaw 46, 124
Gennep 56, 57
General Accident 96, 172
General Assembly 25, 26
General Election 2010 11, 68
Geocaching Mega event 120
George Street, 1–3, 168
Gifford, John 76, 97
Gill, Rt. Hon. Lord 69, 152
Glasgow 9, 26, 29, 32–34, 37, 39, 160
Gleneagles 13
Gloag, Anne 174
Global Conference 42, 44, 171
Golden Charter 32
Golden Jubilee 11, 33
Goldie, Annabel, MSP 145

Golf 75
Gourinchas, M. Le Maire 90
Grant, Brig. C 54
Gray, Jimmy 152
Greyfriars harbour 18, 173
Guildry 14, 62, 88, 125
Guildtown 120
Grubb, Rt. Hon George 139

Haikou, China 49, 84, 154
Hall, Derek 93
Hall marks 126
Harper, Mark MP 141
Harvie, Christopher MSP 69
Heather garden 43
Heart of Scotland Air Show 115
Heather honey 39
Hebrides 22
Heraldry Competition 100
Herriot, Alan 50, 56
Herzog, Oberburgermeister 44, 45, 121
High Court 160, 163
Highland Distillers 97, 98
Highland Region 39
Highland Spring 65, 175
Highlander Battalion 154
Hill, David Octavius 76
Historic Scotland 79
Holyrood Palace 24
Homecoming 10, 11, 38, 39, 51, 52, 60, 61, 90
Honours of Scotland 22, 24
Horsecross 102, 103
Hosie, Stewart MP 69
House of Commons 68
House of Glenorchy 75
Hughes, Dr Peter 44
Hume, David 75
Hutchison, Ian 88, 177
Hyslop, Fiona MSP 73

Iona 15
Irons, Jim 159
Isle of Mann 22
Inglis William 75
Inverness 9, 11, 29, 33, 37, 134, 152, 161
Irwin, Sir Alastair 144, 146
Isaacs, Jeremy 121

Jambouree Choir 96, 97, 152
James Hutton Institute 130
Jameson, Brig. Melville 52, 54, 69, 82, 85, 149

Jameson, George (artist) 74
Johan Victoria 104
Johnnie Walker championship 120

Kay, Billy 119
Kilt pin 125
Kilt run 155, 156
King Alexander I 19
King Alexander III 22, 34
King Charles I 33
King Constantine II 18,
King David I 20–22, 62
King Drosten 16
King Edward I (of England) 17, 22
King Edward VII 29
King Girie 17
King Haakon IV (of Norway) 22
King Henry VIII (of England) 23, 28
King James I 14, 23, 24, 34, 35
King James VI 23, 32 144
King James VI Hospital 23
King John Baliol 22,
King Kenneth MacAlpin 9, 15, 16, 19, 28
King Magnus VI (Norway) 22
King Malcolm III (Canmore) 73
King Robert III 34
King Robert the Bruce 18, 34
King William I, (The Lion) 10, 14, 20, 22, 27
King William The Lion Charter 14, 20, 22, 32, 58, 60, 63, 74, 137
King's Arms Close 167
Kinfauns 138
Kinnoull church 106
Kinnoull primary school 82
Kinross 27
Knight's Cross 124
Kohima Memorial 57
Konstanty Dombrowicz 48

Lade 19, 20
Lady in Blue 75
Lancaster 29
Langer, Guidon 123
Lawson, Rev. Derek 85
Legacy 165–170
Leicester 29
Leishman, Mark 69
Letford, John 140, 152
Letters Patent 12, 29, 157
Light Night Festival 96, 104–107
Lindsay, Lord Jamie 69
Linklater, Baroness Veronica 60, 61, 69, 70, 132, 134

Linlithgow 25
Local Government (Scotland) 14, 162, 163
Loch Leven Castle 27
Lochhead, Richard MSP 68
Locket Book 14, 89
Logan, Bishop Vincent 85
London 23, 61, 63, 71
Long Gallery 82
Lord Chancellor 71
Lord Dean of Guild 14, 15, 84, 86
Lord Lieutenancy 164
Lord John Murray House 129
Lord Lyon 26, 27, 28
Lord Mayoralty 70
Lord Provost 9, 14, 15, 20, 70, 134, 159–164
Lorraine Law 126
Lyon, Lord 162

MacCormick, Provost Jean 50
MacDonald, Dr Alan 94
MacFarlane, Lord, of Bearsden 144
Mackie's Crisps 180
MacNicol, Elizabeth (Bessie) 103
Maciver, Ruaraig 98
Mandelson, Peter MP 70, 71, 134
Mansefield, Lord and Lady 82, 84, 144, 146
Marks & Spencer 74, 93
Marsh Mellow Street Band 91
Marshall Monument 76
Mausoleum 12, 16, 23, 27, 34
Maxwell, Donald 92
McDiarmid Park 66
McGrogan, Bethany 101
McKeachan, Ann MP 68
McKean, Prof. Charles 94
McMillan, Gordon 69
Medway 133
Mercer family 35
Merlin ERD 177
Michael Moore MP 12
Millennium 33
Miller, Cllr Ian 37, 69, 90, 149
Miller, Cllr Sandy 46
Milton Keynes 133
Miraculating Machine 104
Model Railway Club 112
Moncreiffe Hill 16, 93
Monk's Tower 18
Moon Sculpture 101–103
Moore, Michael 135, 142
Morison, David 76
Morris Leslie group 65, 178

Morrison and Mackay 176
Moot Hill 16, 17, 82
Mundell, David 148, 149
Murphy, Jim MP 69
Murray Royal Hospital 66, 130, 161

National Council of the Scottish Clergy 24
National Galleries of Scotland 74,
Naysmith, Alexander 75
Newcastle 23
Ninewells Hospital 130
North Inch 19, 34, 137
Northern Ireland 11
Northern Isles 22
Nuit Blanche 105

O'Donnell, Gerry 98
Ochil Hills 98
Old Council Chambers 13, 47
Operation Plunder 56
Oram, Richard 93
Orchards 124
Orienteering 122

Paisley 33, 35, 114, 139
Paperweight 83, 89, 90
Park World Tour 120, 122
Parliament (Scottish) 12, 21, 24, 25
Parliament Hall 24
Patel, Lord 69
Peace Child 46
Pearce, Sophie 100
Pearson, Maddie 100
Peat, Sir Michael 69, 70
Perry Mr David 69
Perth, a Place in History 92–96
Perth & District Pipe Band 85, 106, 119, 153
Perth & Kinross District Council 26,
Perth & Kinross Heritage Trust 92–96, 167
Perth Bridge 64
Perth Castle 19
Perth College UHI 39, 49, 66, 125, 128, 179
Perth Common Good Fund 125
Perth Festival of the Arts 117
Perth harbour 25, 173
Perth Film Society 118
Perth High Constables 85
Perth in Bloom 42
Perth Literary and Antiquarian Society 76
Perth Mart 172, 173
Perth meets Perth (reel) 100
Perth Museum & Art Gallery 19, 41, 42, 66, 74, 76, 89, 182

Perth, Ontario 48, 49, 84, 154–156
Perth railway station 77, 78
Perth racecourse 66, 67, 116
Perth Royal Infirmary 66, 67, 131
Perth Sailing Club 183
Perth Show 180
Perth Symphony Orchestra 106, 119
Perth Theatre 41, 165
Perth Youth Orchestra 92, 106, 118, 119
Perth, Western Australia 49
Perth800 Ale 126
Perth800 logo 40
Perth800, (Reel) 99
Perth's economy 174
Perthshire Advertiser 143
Perthshire Arts Association 104
Perthshire Brass 119
Perthshire on a Plate 90
Perthshire Photographic Society 113
Perthshire Society of Natural Science 113
Peterson, Sarah 83, 90
Picts 15, 16, 20, 93
Pilgrim Badge 74
Pillar Sculptures 97, 153, 154
Poland 123, 124
Polish Medical School (Edinburgh) 46, 123, 124
Polish military cemetery 46
Polish war memorial 46
Pomarium 125
Portsmouth 29
Prince Charles 59, 69, 77–83, 116, 144, 159
Prince Edward 59, 77, 83–90, 137
Princess Royal 59, 77, 129
Prince's Regeneration Trust 79
Pskov 45, 84, 153
Pullar, Sir Robert 95

Queen, HM The 114, 157
Queen Joan Beaufort 23
Queen Margaret Tudor 23
Queen Victoria 29

Raeburn, Henry 75
Rainbow coalition 12
Ramm, Jessica 104
Ramsay, Allan 75
Reading 133, 141, 148, 149
Reformation 23, 35
Reid, Sir George 143
Rhine crossing 56
Rideau Canal, Canada 48
Riding of the Parliament 24

River Earn 19
River Tay 105, 106
RNLI 65
Robert Douglas Memorial School 82
Robertson, Alexander Duff (artist) 18
Rochester 133
Rome 24
Rotary Clubs 39
Roxburgh 19, 21
Royal Air Force Association 58
Royal British Legion (Scotland) 55, 58, 88, 154
Royal Burghs 9, 14, 19–22
Royal Court 12, 14, 19, 24
Royal Mile 24
Royal Perth Golfing Society 66
Royal Regiment of Scotland 50, 81, 86, 154
Royal Scottish Country Dance Society 98
Royal Scottish Geographical Society 39, 67, 69, 128
Royal Scots Dragoon Guards 51, 52

Salford 29
Salmond, Alex 59, 69, 116, 137, 141, 142, 145, 159
Salutation Hotel 180
Sawers, Dr Lesley 169
Scandinavia 20
Scarlett's of Meigle 40, 180
Schijndel 50, 51
Scone 9, 15–17, 19, 23, 28, 93, 138
Scone Abbey 74
Scone Palace 16, 82, 83, 182
Scott, Provost Bob 45,
Scott, Euna 127
Scott, Sir Walter 9, 33, 168
Scott, Tavish MSP 145
Scottish and Southern Energy 65, 104, 175
Scottish Aero Club 179
Scottish Charities Air Ambulance 178, 179
Scottish Country Dancing 99
Scottish Parliament 23, 60
Scottish Executive 12
Scottish National Party 11,
Scottish Office 68
Scottish Tides – Polish Spring 119
Scotts 15, 20
Second City 9, 14, 24, 28, 63
Secretary of State for Scotland 33
Shanghai 103
Sheriff Court 65
Simon Howie 180
Six Cities Alliance 168–170

Skin & Bone Exhibition 73, 89, 96
Slim, Viscount William 57
Smith, Alyn MEP 44
Smout, Prof. TC 93
Soutar, Sir Brian 174
South Inch 34
Southhampton 30
Spectraglass 177
Spessart Highlanders 84, 85, 153, 154
Spitfire 88, 177
Stagecoach 104, 174
Stephen, Peter 152
Stirling 132, 134, 161
Strachan, David 93, 96
Strang, Gilbert 145
STV 69
St Andrews 36
St Andrew's Day 61, 107
St Asaph 149
St David's Cathedral 31
St Giles Cathedral 33
St John's Centre 74
St John's Kirk 18, 19, 34, 35, 41, 55, 57, 66,
   80, 93, 105, 126, 127, 156, 182
St Johnstone Football Club 66, 117
St Machar's Cathedral 34
St Ninian's Cathedral 36, 41, 182
St Patrick's Anglican cathedra 31
St Patrick's RC cathedral 30
St Petersburg 105
St.William of Perth 133
St Valery-en-caux 56
Stagecoach 65
Stanley Mills 78, 79
Stanners Island 18, 19
Statistical Account of Perth 32,
Stiftsbasilika Kinderchor 118
Stirling 9, 11, 12, 20, 21, 25, 28, 33, 37, 152
Stoke on Trent 29
Stone of Destiny 17, 22
Strathclyde 15
Strathcona cup 111
Straw, Jack MP 71
Sturgeon, Nicola 9, 142, 169
Summer Harvest Oil 80, 180
Sunderland 30
Swan and the Tay (Strathspey) 100
Swansea 30
Swinney, John MSP 79, 140, 183

Tapestry 55, 56
Tay and Earn Trust 183
Tay Descent 110, 165

Tay Estuary 24, 25
Tavish, Scott MSP 25
Territorials 81
The Scots' Crisis of Confidence 44
Thomson, Mr Murray 69
Thurso, Lord John MP 67, 68, 69, 140
Time Capsule 58, 59
Times 149
Tornado, G4 88, 115
Tournai marble slab 35
Trads 120
Travel 'bug' 121
Trailblazers' Exhibition 103
Treaty of Perth 22, 25
Tristan and Isolde, Legend 74
Tullibardine malt whisky 40
Twinning 42, 45, 46, 122

Union of Parliaments 25

Vector Aerospace 65, 176
Verschuur, Mary 94
Veterans Associations 58
View of Perth from Boatland 76
Vine, John 69, 143
VisitScotland 37
Vortex Band 97

Wales 11, 29
Wallace, Rev. Jim 85
Wang Yuyang 101–103
Wars of Independence 22, 23
Warsaw Village Band 119
Weeping Window 166
Whatley, Prof. Christopher 94
Whisky 96, 144, 171
William Wallace 23
Wills, Michael, MP 61, 68, 69
Wishart, Pete MP 60, 61, 63, 69, 70, 138,
   140, 148
Westminster 11, 60–63, 70
Westminster Dinner 68–71
White Trillium 84
Willowgatre 183
Woodend 18
World Curling Federation 66

York Place, 20, 168
Young, Alan 106
Young, Angela 99
Young Lady in a Sun Bonnet 103
York, Duke & Duchess of 76

Some other books published by **LUATH** PRESS

Perth: A Comprehensive Guide for Locals & Visitors

John Hulbert

ISBN: 978-1-910021-43-9 PBK £12.99

This is the first comprehensive guide to the ancient city of Perth. Closely examining each area of the city, John Hulbert explores the institutions, trades, traditions and people that have contributed to Perth's development from the earliest settlement on the site through to the present day. Complete with full colour photographs and maps, the guide provides a detailed overview of Perth's history and its role in wider Scottish and international contexts. It is also an excellent celebration of the city's architecture and public art.

John Hulbert shares his knowledge and experience from nearly 20 years' service on Perth & Kinross Council, including five years as the Provost. Having successfully campaigned to re-instate Perth's city status in 2012, his passion for Scotland's 'fair city' shines through in this compelling and practical guide which will prove invaluable to locals and visitors alike.

How over five centuries ago could the game of tennis play a significant part in Perth's history? Read this book and you will discover how that happened and on the way you will also discover many other facets of the city's fascinating history as well as a wealth of information about life in Perth today.

From the Foreword by MARK WEBSTER, former Chairman of The Gannochy Trust

Perth: A City Again

Jeremy Duncan

ISBN: 978-1-908373-56-4 PBK £14.99

So, with a great sense of hope, and some sadness, and with the concerns, successes and failures of everyday folk, Perth set off on what blurb writers might describe as a roller-coaster ride of ups and downs, twists and jolts, through the 20th century.

In 2012, the ancient honour of Perth was restored when it became a city again. Jeremy Duncan narrates Perth's journey from city to town and back again, providing a revealing insight into the character of Perth and its people. With a collection of archive and modern images and newspaper reports, Duncan's thoroughly researched account covers every aspect of Perth life taking the reader on a remarkable journey from past to present.

If you live in Edinburgh, getting to the Highlands is a hassle, and vice versa; but if you live in Perth, in the heart of Scotland, you feel as if you have the whole country at your beck and call.

THE TELEGRAPH

Details of these and other books published by Luath Press can be found at: **www.luath.co.uk**

Luath Press Limited
committed to publishing well written books worth reading

LUATH PRESS takes its name from Robert Burns, whose little collie Luath (*Gael.,* swift or nimble) tripped up Jean Armour at a wedding and gave him the chance to speak to the woman who was to be his wife and the abiding love of his life.

Burns called one of 'The Twa Dogs' Luath after Cuchullin's hunting dog in Ossian's *Fingal*. Luath Press was established in 1981 in the heart of Burns country, and now resides a few steps up the road from Burns' first lodgings on Edinburgh's Royal Mile.

Luath offers you distinctive writing with a hint of unexpected pleasures.

Most bookshops in the UK, the US, Canada, Australia, New Zealand and parts of Europe either carry our books in stock or can order them for you. To order direct from us, please send a £sterling cheque, postal order, international money order or your credit card details (number, address of cardholder and expiry date) to us at the address below. Please add post and packing as follows: UK – £1.00 per delivery address; overseas surface mail – £2.50 per delivery address; overseas airmail – £3.50 for the first book to each delivery address, plus £1.00 for each additional book by airmail to the same address. If your order is a gift, we will happily enclose your card or message at no extra charge.

Luath Press Limited
543/2 Castlehill
The Royal Mile
Edinburgh EH1 2ND
Scotland

Telephone: 0131 225 4326 (24 hours)
email: sales@luath.co.uk
Website: www.luath.co.uk